EVOLUTIONARY CONSCIOUSNESS

EVOLUTIONARY CONSCIOUSNESS

The Dream of Life

---

by Wayne Omura

Bäuu Press
Golden, CO

ISBN: 978-19-36955-22-0

Designed by Nathaniel Kennon Perkins
Cover photo: Type 1a supernova explosion.

Published by Bäuu Press
Golden, CO
www.bauuinstitute.com

For the dreams forgotten

as we sleep through life.

CONTENTS

FOREWORD

Upon her deathbed, my great-grandmother, Marie Metz Koning (1868-1926), managed to scrawl on a piece of paper "Ik droomde," which is Dutch for "I dreamed." Then she passed away. My grandmother, who was at her side, treasured that piece of paper all her life. When she showed it to me we wondered what those enigmatic words really meant. Had Marie realized that her life had been one long dream? After all, as a famous author in the early 20th century, a writer of beautifully allegorical novels that hinted at the underlying mystery of everyday experience, her stories hinted at a dream world. Clearly, she really wanted to communicate just one more time what she was experiencing in that moment at the very edge of eternity.

Wayne Omura now guides us along an extraordinary journey that bridges a world between dreams and waking life, a realm that makes us question what we know about reality. He has delved deeply into the nature of the dream world, which seems to be inextricably bound up with what we call conscious existence. A glance at the chapter headings is enough to draw you in as he outlines how countless writers, philosophers and scientists have confronted the meaning of what seems to be a dream world of experience. Just what is real? Can we trust our senses? And what should we make of the physicist's discoveries concerning the realm of quantum effects that fly in the face of common sense. Based on an astonishing amount of research into a vast range of topics that touch upon the theme of his book, Omura sweeps you along as he ties together such disparate topics as wave-particle duality, consciousness and lucid dreaming.

I first met Wayne in 1978 when he was a student in an introductory astronomy course I taught at the University of Colorado in Boulder. He was one of 220 students but quickly stood out as being totally different. His potential talent was revealed when he handed in an essay on relativity. I was expecting 10 pages and he handed in 50 pages and the content was astonishing.* Instead of writing an essay referencing well-known facts about relativity, he explored what he believed to be its foundations and implications without any equations and drew his own general conclusions. He came oh so close to the insights associated with Einstein's work. I suspected that had Wayne been endowed with a natural skill in mathematical physics he might possibly have completed the task of formalizing the essence of relativity.

Back then Wayne was young and enthusiastic, always bent on learning in his own unique way. Now he has matured but he is still driven to understand the underlying truths of existence. He has devoted his life to this quest and in *Evolutionary Consciousness* he sweeps the reader along to visit not just the world of dreams, but also that world in which scientists struggle with the concept that we live in a universe where our existence, as observers, plays a fundamental role in determining the nature of reality. After all, what are we to make of those experiments that have demonstrated that two particles moving away from their point of origin remain inextricably and instantaneously linked no matter how far apart they may fly? And can we truly wrap our imaginations around the odd behavior of light as either a particle or a wave, and how it appears that the observer has the ultimate say in determining which property is manifested, and when.

The format of Evolutionary Consciousness reminds me of a book that deeply impressed me as a teenager. It was The Outsider by Colin Wilson, a compendium of the thoughts of many philosophers, but Wilson left me with little sense of what it all meant. Wayne has done a lot more than collect ideas. He weaves his own insights in with those of many other thinkers into a coherent whole. His tale allows me to better understand what my great-grandmother confronted as she lay

*The essay was "Through the Cosmic Looking-Glass: The Relativistic Nature of Energy and Light" and is now included in my book Alcheringa: A Metaphysical Alchemy. It proposes that the universe is accelerating in its expansion at velocities that surpass the speed of light. In 2011 astronomers Perlmutter, Schmidt, and Riess were awarded the Nobel Prize for their study of Type 1A supernovae in distant galaxies. Their study proved the universe was actually accelerating its expansion at velocities possibly greater than the speed of light. This also provided further evidence for the existence of dark energy which seems to be necessary to propel the universe at such an accelerating expansion. Vera Rubin's study of mass distribution in spiral galaxies was the complementary evidence supporting the existence of dark matter: there was not enough visible matter in galaxies to keep them from flying apart.

dying. Her dying words may indeed have carried meaning that we can barely grasp. As she faded she saw something that must have been awe inspiring, so momentous that she struggled, literally with her last breath, to tell her daughter what she had sensed. It is that dream-like aspect of life, and the unreality of the many strange, counter-intuitive discoveries of modern physics that point to the possibility that there exists in our universe much more than we have dreamed of in our philosophies.

As you read Omura's story, you will be changed. We are all connected in mysterious ways. Just as we cannot observe an atom without altering its motion or position, so you won't be able to read this book and remain unchanged. What you then do with what Omura reveals is entirely up to you. Or is it?

-- Gerrit L. Verschuur, Ph.D.

Radio astronomer and author of, among other titles, *Hidden Attraction: The History and Mystery of Magnetism, The Invisible Universe: The Story of Radio Astronomy* and *Is Anyone Out There?: Personal Adventures in the Search for Extraterrestrials.*

INTRODUCTION

Is reality a dream? Are dreams real? Man is on the verge of a reconception of the universe. Advances in physics, cosmology, physiology, and psychology reveal an underlying principle governing life. This principle will be the catalyst in the evolution of human consciousness.

What is the purpose of life? What is really real? Mankind has been plagued by such questions and doubts. A subtle uneasiness has pervaded the metaphysical air—a feeling that something was missing, that somehow all had not been said. And yet the answer to man's dilemma lay within his own mind, within the darkness of his own imaginings, within the solitude of his own dream. Man's questioning was itself the answering which he sought.

How does consciousness affect the perception of reality? Does consciousness in any way alter, shape, or determine reality? Can purely subjective experience manifest itself in the objective world? Are dreams as real as life? Are they consciously valid experiences? Can man, in the final analysis, dream his own dream—create his own reality? Or is reality, in the long run, inexorably static and absolute—totally beyond the influence of the subjective mind?

Because life cannot be approached one-dimensionally, neither can reality. The structure of this book is holistic and many-dimensional. The interdisciplinary view shows the universe in its many-faceted light. It is a holographic diamond viewed from different angles and perspectives.

The journey is argumentative. One explores, comes to understanding and realizations. Contradictions are investigated and resolved. The vision is formed and refined—tempered until it crystallizes into clarity.

Experiments in sleep, dreams, altered states of consciousness, and perception will be evaluated from the psychophysiological aspects of consciousness. Stories and novels will be juxtaposed and cited as the possible metaphysical ramifications of such work. Philosophical speculations will be posed as challenging frameworks for living life. And finally, relativity, quantum mechanics, and string theory, as well as cosmological theories and astrophysical evidence will demonstrate the tentative and relative nature of reality.

The concluding premise is that subjective perception somehow determines objective reality, that the universe is somewhat malleable and in flux, that it is our mode of perception which determines, not only our own subjective reality, but also the objective reality of the world at large.

PART ONE

The Reality of a Dream

"Dreams are true while they last.

Can we, at the best, say more of life?" [1]

—*Havelock Ellis*

1. Havelock Ellis, <u>The World of Dreams</u> (Boston and New York: Houghton Mifflin Company, 1922), p. 281.

Dreams as a Form of Life

"Life, what is it but a dream?"[2]
—*Lewis Carroll*

Is life simply a dream? Man has pondered this question since the dawn of time. Since the first proto-man awoke from a strange, perhaps terrifying dream, the riddle has been posed, and yet remains unsolved. Was it real? Could dreams somehow be true? And consequently with this unsettling dilemma came the inevitable question: what is real? Is reality itself really real? Could reality be a dream? Is life really nothing but a dream? Each and every human being encounters the horror of this enigma. As a child one may awaken with a scream, shaking with tears and sobs of anguish, only to hear a comforting voice repeating calmly with sympathy that, "It was only a dream . . ."

Will this also occur in the transition beyond death? Will one awaken to a voice saying softly that none of it was real? Perhaps. But does it make any difference to the child with the nightmare? To one who has suffered the torments of hell, does it matter how the experience is labeled? For to the dreamer the dream was the ultimate experience, perhaps far more real than anything else in his life. The child knows inwardly that the explanation is a lie, for he instinctively senses the reality of dreams. Yet the dream is too frightening and too terrible to accept. Willfully, and with clever self-deception, the child pretends with the lies and games. Lying comfortably with security and warmth, the child also considers the dream as unreal.

---

2. Lewis Carroll, <u>Through the Looking- Glass: and what Alice found there</u> (New York: Random House, Inc., 1946), p. 166.

5

But what if it isn't? What if this universal experience common to all men just happens to be real? Or at least a link to the real (real in the sense of being somehow metaphysically or spiritually valid)? Such is the belief of many "primitive" tribes and cultures. According to British anthropologist Francis Huxley:

> An Indian of the Gran Chaco of Argentina once accused
> a missionary of stealing his pumpkins. At the time of the
> theft the missionary had been two hundred miles away, but
> the Indian knew him to be guilty because he had seen it all
> in a dream. Many other stories from this part of the world
> show how quick Indians have been to accept dreams as true,
> and in similar situations have killed suspects who were in
> fact innocent—of the act, if not of the intention. Dreamers
> in this state have no touchstone by which to discern the
> difference between the image of reality and the reality of
> an image . . .[3]

Thus dreams and reality become one and the same—each as valid as the other. But what is surprising is that modern dream research lends credence to these "primitive" views.

Dreams were formerly considered either a product of subconscious processes or else a by-product of random physiological discharges within the brain. In either case they were a mere fantasy play of thoughts and images resulting from the conscious mind's apparent state of rest. Dreams held no true conscious experience, for they were purely a result of the mind or ego's impairment, a loss of reason, and a lack of control. And thus man's imagination was justified in performing the most monstrous deeds.

Hatred, violence, murder, and torture. Anything was allowed, for "it was only a dream." The depravity was shuffled off to some elusive specter. The subconscious was responsible. It was the "id" and not "I." Dreams were viewed only as a personal quirk, an idiosyncrasy, and a blowing off of steam. They were merely the flow of psychic content, curious for a moment, but not really authentic. Courage and bravery or cowardice and fear. Pleasure, pain, happiness, or despair. It made no difference, for it was all imaginary—isolated and apart from the conscious reality of life.

But sleep laboratory research has uncovered some astonishing

3. Francis Huxley, The Way of the Sacred (New York: Doubleday and Company, Inc., 1974), p. 49.

facts. The REM (rapid eye movement) period of intense dream sleep coincides not with general brain deactivation as was previously assumed, but rather with a highly aroused reactivation! Autonomic functions soar to the peak of their nighttime sleep, corresponding closely to that of waking consciousness. Rather than resulting from the brain's period of rest, most dreams occur during a high state of physiological arousal.* Brain waves increase in frequency till nearly indistinguishable from waves of normal, active waking consciousness. Conjugate eye movements occur in sporadic bursts, making it appear as though the dreamer were actually watching his dream. From all indications the dreamer should be awake, and yet he is perhaps further from this world than at any other time in his life.

Because of its puzzling and contradictory nature the REM dream period has earned the name "paradoxical sleep." William Dement, a pioneer in dream research, explains that because of these paradoxical observations, "There is some speculation that REM sleep is not really sleep at all, but a state in which the subject is awake, but paralyzed and hallucinating." [4]

This conclusion is further corroborated by studies on evoked potentials during REM. The evidence indicates that such evoked potentials tend to be low. And thus, according to physiologist Ernest Hartmann, "the D-state shows a remarkable similarity to an active, distracted waking state." [5] Further evidence comes from research on somniloquy or sleep-talking. According to psychologist Arthur Arkin, speech patterns show significant differences between REM and non-REM sleep.

> When associated with REM sleep, they were somewhat more likely to be correct in syntax, inflection and word structure. Almost all cases of marked abnormality were associated with NREM sleep . . . [6]

The controversy between REM and non-REM mentation is still plagued with misunderstanding and contradictions. Dream mentation does occur during non-REM sleep. However, the general consensus is that classical, "active" dreams do correspond to the REM period, with less active, less emotional, more thought-like mentation occurring during non-REM sleep.

4. William C. Dement, Some Must Watch While Some Must Sleep (Stanford: Stanford Alumni Association, 1972), p. 26.
5. Ernest Hartmann, The Biology of Dreaming (Springfield, Illinois: Charles C. Thomas, 1967), p. 38.
6. Arthur M. Arkin, The Mind in Sleep (Hillsdale, New Jersey: Lawrence Erlbaum Associates, Inc., Publishers, 1978), p. 521.

Thus mental processes themselves tend to be more or less intact during REM as opposed to being somewhat impaired during non-REM. Such intriguing discoveries have led many researchers to consider REM sleep as "an entirely different state of existence"—totally distinguishable from either waking consciousness or non-REM sleep. Psychiatrist Frederick Snyder goes so far as to conclude:

> The physiological characteristics of this phenomenon prove so distinctive that I consider it a third state of earthly existence, the rapid eye movement or REM State, which is at least as different from sleeping and waking as each is from the other . . . [8]

And what's more, Snyder is so impressed by the realistic aspect of dreaming that he regards it as a state perhaps more powerful than waking consciousness.

> Such considerations have led me to suggest that dreaming might best be defined simply as a state of being alive in a hallucinated reality, and that perhaps in some ways we are more intensely alive in our dreaming than in our waking existence. [9]

Thus the idea returns, but now in a respectable form. Perhaps dreams are a valid conscious experience, and not merely random discharges or the ramblings of the subconscious mind. This "absurd" notion could be regarded as fantasy, were it not for its unsettling basis in fact. The metaphysical validity of dreams has found support within the very framework of science—the most objective measure of reality and life.

In the light of these findings, primitive man may have had a better grasp of the truth than his modern-day counterpart. According to many ancient and modern myths and religions, dreams are an alternate dimension, a state where the soul detaches from the body, wandering freely throughout the spiritual plane, commingling with both spirits

7. Dement, op. cit., p. 26.
8. Frederick Snyder, "Toward an Evolutionary Theory of Dreaming," The American Journal of Psychiatry, August 1966, Volume 123, Number 2, p. 121.
9. Frederick Snyder, "In Quest of Dreaming," Experimental Studies of Dreaming, Herman A. Witkin & Helen B. Lewis (editors), (New York: Random House, Inc., 1967), p. 39.

and demons, and even capable of communion with the dead. While this may be a somewhat fanciful view, it may still paint a more accurate portrait of dreams than modern man's flippant disregard. But rather than succumbing to occult mysticism, let us approach the subject in a more philosophical light.

If dreams are real, then what is the nature of this strange reality? Is it simply a wonderland of phantasmagoria where the characters and inhabitants just happen to be real? If this is true and there is nothing more to dreams than simple reality, then what is there to distinguish dreams from life? Is it enough to say dreams are as real as life, when life may in turn be nothing more than a dream? Such circular definitions and circular reasoning sends one spiraling into an absurd universe. One becomes lost in the madhouse of undifferentiated truth. Alice is herself accosted by this unsettling dilemma, and in the chess game of life nearly forfeits her soul to a Looking-Glass dream. Referring to the Red King snoring peacefully upon the ground:

> "He's dreaming now," said Tweedledee: "and what do you think he's dreaming about?"
>
> Alice said "Nobody can guess that."
>
> "Why, about you!" Tweedledee exclaimed, clapping his hands triumphantly. "And if he left off dreaming about you, where do you suppose you'd be?"
>
> "Where I am now, of course," said Alice.
>
> "Not you!" Tweedledee retorted contemptuously. "You'd be nowhere. Why, you're only a sort of thing in his dream!"
>
> "If that there King was to wake," added Tweedledum, "you'd go out—bang!—just like a candle!"
>
> "I shouldn't!" Alice exclaimed indignantly.
>
> "Besides, if I'm only a sort of thing in his dream, what are you, I should like to know?"
>
> "Ditto," said Tweedledum.
>
> "Ditto, ditto!" cried Tweedledee.
>
> He shouted this so loud that Alice couldn't help saying "Hush! You'll be waking him, I'm afraid, if you make so much noise."
>
> "Well, it's no use your talking about waking him," said Tweedledum, "when you're only one of the things in his dream. You know very well you're not real."
>
> "I am real!" said Alice, and began to cry.

> "You won't make yourself a bit realler by crying,"
> Tweedledee remarked: "there's nothing to cry about."
>
> "If I wasn't real," Alice said—half laughing
> through her tears, it all seemed so ridiculous—"I
> shouldn't be able to cry."
>
> "I hope you don't suppose those are <u>real</u> tears?"
> Tweedledum interrupted in a tone of great contempt.
>
> "I know they're talking nonsense," Alice thought
> to herself: "and it's foolish to cry about it." So she
> brushed away her tears, and went on as cheerfully as
> she could . . ." [10]

As cheerfully as she could! Alice has indeed the greatest courage of all. With Faustian defiance and Promethean courage she succeeds in asserting the reality of her dream—her <u>own</u> dream. Facing madness and possible nonexistence, Alice maintains her validity, and so secures her dream-soul. With the stubborn dignity of a defiant child she refuses defeat, for defeat would entail removal from the board, and as far as she was concerned, an end to the game. As it is, even a stalemated argument allows continued play with hope for victory, while conceding would have meant losing her soul, expiring as was warned, in a puff of smoke. The Tweedle brothers were correct as far as they themselves were concerned. They indeed were nothing more than a figment of a dream, and so too was Alice, for her dream-self was also merely an image from her mind. But the Red King?—that is the question of all questions. Is he the reality behind all dreams? Or simply the dream of a dreamer's dream? The riddle, of course, will remain unsolved.

When dreams become just as real as life, reality can in turn become nothing more than a dream. Without distinction one is lost within a labyrinth of mere appearance, bereft of any contrasting frame of reference. The world becomes unreal as dreams assume the role of a mocking parody of life. Existence is rendered meaningless, and one is confused and alone, abandoned to the haunting reality of an empty dream. What would it be like if this were true? How would one feel? How would one act? Mark Twain's Satan, <u>The Mysterious Stranger</u>, in conversation about the true nature of the world:

---

10. Lewis Carroll, <u>Through the Looking-Glass: and what Alice found there</u> (New York: Random House, Inc., 1946), pp. 63-64.

"It was a vision—it had no existence."
I could hardly breathe for the great hope that was
struggling in me—
"A vision?—a vi--"
"Life itself is only a vision, a dream."
It was electrical. By God I had had that very
thought a thousand times in my musings!
"Nothing exists; all is a dream. God—man—the
world,--the sun, the moon, the wilderness of stars: a
dream, all a dream, they have no existence." . . .
"Strange! that you should not have suspected,
years ago, centuries, ages, aeons ago! for you have
existed, companionless, through all the eternities.
Strange, indeed, that you should not have suspected
that your universe and its contents were only dreams,
visions, fictions! Strange, because they are so frankly
and hysterically insane—like all dreams" . . .

And in the mounting climax to this horrifying revelation:

"It is true, that which I have revealed to you: there
is no God, no universe, no human race, no earthly
life, no heaven, no hell. It is all a Dream, a grotesque
and foolish dream. Nothing exists but You. And
You are but a Thought—a vagrant Thought, a useless
Thought, a homeless Thought, wandering forlorn
among the empty eternities!" He vanished, and left
me appalled; for I knew, and realized, that all he had
said was true. [11]

Is this how it will end? Is this the climax to all spiritual strife?—a
dreamer lost within the pseudo-reality of his dream, a spiritual outcast
with nowhere to go, an eternal wanderer who has lost his soul. Twain's
biting cynicism for the human race reaches its ultimate expression
within this last, unfinished book. Satan is cast in the role of a nihilistic
prophet of doom, revealing to the world a vision of utter desolation.
Embittered by the cruel absurdity of life, Twain strikes back with a
vengeful, soul-searing cry: Life is an illusion, and nothing is real!
When dreams and reality intertwine, one can lose all meaningful

---

11. Mark Twain, The Mysterious Stranger (Berkeley and Los Angeles, California:
University of California Press, 1969), pp. 404-405.

perspective on existence. The world becomes a Wonderland of living madness where everyday life is nothing more than another real dream. And when dreams become the only reality, one becomes lost within a spiritual abyss. The world assumes an aura of meaningless chaos, and nihilism thus becomes the only rational response. For if the universe is only a lunatic dream, then only a madman would continue to accord it meaning.

In this way, the possible reality of dreams casts an ominous shadow upon the metaphysical value of life. But this is so only if dreams are merely a mindless reality as meaningless as a bedlam of kooks. The assumption, though not necessarily false, is also not necessarily true. More evidence is required before a verdict can be reached, for perhaps there is more to dreams than meets the eye. Perhaps there is some mysterious force, some deeper intelligence, controlling or guiding our subconscious life.

Passing "Through the Looking-Glass" into Alice's dream we are fated once again to meet the sleeping Red King. Were the Tweedle brothers correct about the nature of the King? Is he the unknown factor within the equation of life? Is this comical character from Looking-Glass world simply a playing-piece image of Alice's dream? Or, through the image of the sleeping Red King, does Alice catch a glimpse of subconscious reality—the subliminal force behind all dreams, the true player in the awesome chess game of life?

Carroll himself teases the reader with this tantalizing dilemma, ending his book with the chapter, "Which Dreamed It?" and concluding his story with the words, "Which do you think it was?" In other words, was the Red King a figment of Alice's dream? Or was Alice the figment of the Red King's dream? The problem is one of establishing identity. Could it be that there is a deeper essence responsible for our inner world of dreams? Is it possible that some strange, perhaps alien force is controlling and dominating our subconscious life? This Red King enigma must first be assessed with regard to the intrinsic nature of dreams.

The Dream Force

What is questioned is not the existence of a fundamental subconscious force. Sigmund Freud, followed by other schools of psychotherapy, has already demonstrated this secret aspect of our "self"—tinkering away on a lower level of awareness, puttering about in the dusty corners of our mind. The existence of the subconscious has been firmly established. What is questioned is the possibility of an alien force (alien, meaning something beyond man's conscious or even subconscious nature) somehow affecting, perhaps even residing within the dormant regions of man's mind. The distinction is between a domestic force concerned only with personal and emotional needs, and a force of a completely outré nature operating furtively for some arcane reason.

The problem is not as simple as it seems, for even the familiar subconscious is vague and not yet clearly understood. Even though psychotherapists and psychologists might argue otherwise, the structure of the mind is still fraught with mystery. Modern psychology has scarcely penetrated the gloomy regions of the mind: the powers of hypnosis, meditation, and trance—the enigma of mental illness, behavior disorders, sleep, dreams, and drugs. The entire realm of the subconscious is still open to speculation. Explanations are unsatisfying. Theories are rife. No general consensus on the subliminal world can be formed, for consciousness research has just begun.

The only certainty is that the subconscious exists. Whether it is merely a hidden aspect of our personality, or whether an independent force from beyond—no one can say, and no one would dare. And so any evidence, no matter how startling, is simply attributed to the subconscious mind. And thus its status has grown through the years, from a secluded entity playing with mental illness and dreams to a formidable power source of creativity and wisdom. All that is known for certain is that something strange is coexisting—a force so awesome that it can obliterate consciousness, blinding through dreams one's perception of life. It can even force sleepwalkers to wander unconsciously through the world. (And perhaps this is symbolic for man's role in life.) It can remember perfectly the past, dominate through sickness the present, and by stressful inner conflict alter decisions on the future. Through hypnosis it can allow one to relive past experiences, to descend through the years and to become a mere child. Through hypnosis the subconscious can deactivate pain, paralyze the body, and completely disorient the functional structure of the mind. The mysteries are endless and the power immense. As the subconscious outgrows its alter ego limits it more closely approaches the nature of an independent mind. And from an independent mind one should expect certain discrepancies, for there would be two conscious forces instead of just one.

Perhaps the most tangible evidence for the existence of this force are the brain-wave recordings of the EEG. According to Gibbs & Gibbs, the most prominent pioneers of electroencephalography, two sets of brain waves often appear during normal adult sleep; the sleep of infants (which is mostly deep sleep); the seizure patterns of epileptics; as well as in a comprehensive study of subjects under anesthesia.[12] During the calm and quiescent period of deep sleep or other slow-wave phenomena, the high-amplitude, low-frequency normal delta waves are superimposed by low-amplitude, fast waves of another source. It is possible, perhaps even probable, that these strange dual waves coexist at all times, but only become apparent as the brain slows for rest. For the nature of the EEG makes them impossible to detect while the mind is in an actively conscious state. While not conclusive proof of an "alien consciousness," this evidence, at the very least, exemplifies the strange duality of the mind.

Having explored the psychological aspects of subliminal consciousness, let us expand our view to the metaphysical plane. What is of interest is not the mere existence of some alternative force, but rather the implications which its existence would entail. What would it reveal as far as the meaning of life is concerned? What about the nature of spiritual reality? Philosophical ramifications for the destiny of man?—alternate dimensions?—the structure of the universe? Let

---

12. Frederick A. Gibbs & Erna L. Gibbs, Atlas of Electroencephalography (Cambridge, Massachusetts: Lew A. Cummings Co., 1941), pp. 2 & 38 (infants), pp. 45-50 (normal adults), p. 76 (epileptics), p. 132 (anesthesia).

us examine these issues in a more philosophical light.

Are dreams not only real, but a link to another form of being—a gateway to another reality? Is this what the Red King represents? Is this why Alice takes her predicament so seriously and breaks down in tears? Does she, a mere pawn, feel intimidated by the omnipotent King? Is her selfhood threatened by this entity who will determine not only the outcome of The Game, but the outcome of her game. For the King is the most valuable player of all—the focal point of the entire labyrinthine game. His existence must be guarded and defended at all costs, for the fate of all chessmen remains in his hands. His slightest disturbance unbalances the game. His slightest danger threatens the pretended reality. But what is the nature of the real reality? If life is a chess game which everyone plays, then what is the nature of the transcendent realm? After all the pieces have been put aside, with what are we left to say, "this is real." What is it Tweedledum warned that the King must not awaken to? Is it simply the empty image of a Looking-Glass world devoid of any reflection of Satan's "illusions of life?" Or is it some alien world beyond human understanding, perhaps frightening or mystical, perhaps demonic or sublime. What will greet the Red King once he awakens from the imaginary chess-dream of life?

The Nightmare of Life

If there is such a trans-dimensional force beyond dreams then what is the nature of this strange, new realm? H.P. Lovecraft, author of chilling horror stories and tales of the macabre:

> The most merciful thing in the world...is the inability of the human mind to correlate all its contents. We live on an island of ignorance in the midst of black seas of infinity, and it was not meant that we should voyage far...[13]

What Lovecraft ominously implies is that madness and horror lie beyond the gateway of the subconscious. Central to his "mythos" and apparent throughout his works is the theme that evil forces are lurking on the threshold of this reality. Outside space and time, coexisting in another dimension, these demonic entities inhabit a frightening reality—a reality which man may contact through the dissociated states of madness and dreams. Lovecraft is cited not because he is an authority on the subject, but simply because his writings represent the quintessential genre of such outré myths and superstitions of the occult. All throughout history, expressed through literature, religion, and the arts, is the idea that evil lurks just beyond this world. Lovecraft may simply be capitalizing on man's grotesque imagination, but more serious writers than he have expressed somewhat similar, though not as diabolical a view of life. Franz Kafka, one of the greatest literary stylists of the twentieth century: "The Dream reveals the reality, which

---

13. H.P. Lovecraft & August Derleth, "The Shadow Out of Space" from <u>The Survivor & Others</u> (New York: Ballantine Books, Inc., 1957), p. 108.

Henry Fuseli. *The Nightmare*. 1781. Detroit Institute of Arts.

conception lags behind. That is the horror of life—the terror of art." [14]

Kafka's novels and stories, notorious for their nightmarish quality, employ a dream-like, surrealistic technique to express man's alienation in an absurd and hostile universe—a logically insane universe which he cannot understand. In Kafka's view, life is a strange sort of dream, radically removed and dissociated from reality.

The Kafkaesque plots, while different, are thematically the same. The central character, the hero and representative of man, enters the story (of life?) as an interpreter of dreams. Baffled by the illogic and menacing absurdity, he eventually succumbs to frustration and anxiety—the gradual metamorphosis of a dream into a nightmare. One finds oneself compelled by strangely irresistible forces to commit suicide by leaping off a bridge; stripped of one's clothing and forced to lie naked beside a dying man with a wound filled with worms; and in the most bizarre instance unnatural dream forces have transformed one's body into a giant bug!

These situations, though frightening in themselves, are not simply Kafkaesque examples of dreams turned into nightmares, but rather a somber reflection of Kafka's own perhaps demented or perhaps enlightened view of life. It is not enough for this modern Sisyphus to posit an inimical force controlling man's inner world of dreams; he also goes so far as to presume that this force is determining man's life. For as Kafka explains, "The dream reveals the reality . . ." And thus he believes that the insanity of dreams is a reflection of life. Whereas real life, on the other hand, also mirrors the world of dreams. The difficulty arises from the ambiguous terminology.

Kafka felt that human life was essentially unreal, simply as a result of its removal or dissociation from the primal source or from the absolute reality. Everyday life and the normally presumed reality is therefore, in effect, actually a dream. Dreams, however, revealing the illusions of life, consequently maintain a greater semblance of the truth, and therefore are a more accurate portrayal of reality. Not the "absolute reality," but the only reality Kafka felt man could know—the elusive dream-world of existential reality. And it is obvious from Kafka's literary oeuvre that he began to suspect and finally came to believe that the "absolute" was in fact the existential dream unreality—that all man could know, that all that existed was the delusive madness of a paradoxically real nightmare.

And so, Kafka's philosophy is perhaps more diabolical than

---

14. Gustav Janouch, <u>Conversations with Kafka</u> (New York: New Directions Publishing Corporation, 1969), pp. 55-56.

Lovecraft's, for the demonic forces waiting just beyond this world are already present and in control of Kafka's pessimistically paranoid and nightmarish world scheme. It must be stressed that this unsettling Weltanschauung is not simply a fictional device for selling books. (Kafka sold very little in his lifetime.) But rather it is the tragic world of frustration and paranoia through which the fragile Franz Kafka attempted to live his life.

Whether true or false does not alter the fact that Kafka suspected his philosophy to be true. Whether he was laboring under a delusion, or whether he was perceiving the truth, makes no difference. For such is the reality in which Kafka lived and died, such is the dream-nightmare of Kafka's own inner life.

In his most terrifying and also his most popular novel, The Trial, Kafka has his hero awaken "one fine morning" to find himself under arrest. He is never formally charged with a crime, but is nevertheless somehow already guilty from the start. All his attempts at a defense are frustrated and in vain, for he has no idea of the actual charge, and therefore cannot possibly ascertain either his innocence or his guilt. All his efforts to understand the "Law" are futile, for in the end, without a hearing or trial, the hero is evidently condemned to death. "On the evening before K.'s thirty-first birthday" he is accosted by two "gentlemen," two "tenth-rate old actors," and taken forcibly to an abandoned quarry where he is stretched upon a boulder for execution.

> Then one of them opened his frock coat and out of a sheath that hung from a belt girt round his waistcoat drew a long, thin, double-edged butcher's knife, held it up, and tested the cutting edge in the moonlight. Once more the odious courtesies began, the first handed the knife across K. to the second, who handed it across K. back again to the first.[15]

And so, with panic and a last desperate attempt at hope, K. wonders whether he will be saved in the end. Is there a hidden meaning to it all? Is there a universal justice to life? Or is reality simply a nightmare of madness and evil?

> Where was the judge whom he had never seen? Where was the High Court, to which he had never penetrated? He raised his hands and spread out all

---

15. Franz Kafka, The Trial (New York: Alfred A. Knopf, Inc., 1956), p. 285.

his fingers.

But the hands of one of the partners were already at K.'s throat, while the other thrust the knife deep into his heart and turned it there twice. With failing eyes K. could still see the two of them immediately before him, cheek leaning against cheek, watching the final act. "Like a dog!" he said; it was as if the shame of it must outlive him.[16]

And so the force controlling both dreams and life reveals itself for what it is: a murderous band of sadistic cutthroats, a nightmare horror inimical to man. It is interesting to note that what Kafka posited as the insidious nature of reality was vindicated through Kafka's own life. After many years of suffering, he died from tuberculosis or consumption—a wasting away of living tissue, a deterioration which literally consumed him alive. Fortunately Kafka died before the crisis which overtook his family. For almost as though in confirmation of his paranoid pessimism, all three of his sisters came to the same fate as Joseph K.—exterminated like rats in Nazi death-camps.

Kafka is not alone in his appraisal of the underpinnings of life— the malevolent aspect of the subconscious or trans-conscious mind. Among twentieth century novelists and playwrights, Samuel Beckett, Eugene Ionesco, and even Joseph Conrad have also expressed somewhat similar views.

In Conrad's most popular story, "Heart of Darkness," the central character (Marlow) embarks upon a symbolic quest into the heart of the darkest continent in the world, the darkness within the heart of man's subconscious or soul, and the universal darkness within the heart of all life. Kurtz, a previous sojourner and former idealist, is found to have been driven mad by this spiritual and psychological descent.

Marlow realizes from his encounter with Kurtz, that human society is based upon false premises and delusions. The truth of man's being lies within the liberation of animalistic instincts. Senseless murder, wanton depravity, sadism, torture, lust and greed—all are the exclusive province of the ultimate Absolute. At the heart of all reality, whether conscious or subconscious, is the decadent madness of pure horror and evil. During a brief moment of lucidity as Kurtz lies dying, his last words of judgment as he cries out "at some image, at some

---

16. Ibid., p. 286.

vision . . . 'The horror! The horror!' " [17]

The question is not whether Lovecraft, Kafka, or Conrad actually believed what they wrote; that itself is irrelevant. What is important is whether their vision is simply fictional reading or metaphysical fact. In other words, is what they write about the trans-conscious realm true? Are there hostile forces at work within man's subconscious or unconscious mind?

Supposing the existence of a malevolent entity, one should then expect to find a tendency toward negative or unpleasant "inner-worldly" experiences. As far as the subconscious world of dreams is concerned, this tendency would result from conflict or contact with the malevolence residing deep within. If dreams are a manifestation of this turmoil, then dreams should be generally unpleasant or bad. And this is apparently just the case. Hall and Nordby, pioneers in the content analysis of dreams, have together studied over 50,000 dreams from across the world, from modern man to primitive aborigine. And as they explain, as far as the subjective experience of dreams is concerned:

> It has been established by our investigations that dreams of misfortune outnumber dreams of good fortune. Many more bad things than good things happen to the dreamer in his dreams. We have never found an exception to this rule for individual dreams or groups of dreams, nor for female or male dream series. [18]

The results of over 50,000 dream reports cannot be ignored. Nor can it be ignored that these samplings were made from a wide variety of diverse cultures and age groups—a universal sampling of true dream nature, as it were. Nordby and Hall further point out that the Freudian interpretation of dream motivation has now been disproved. Dreams obviously cannot be motivated by the pleasure principle or wish-fulfillment, for otherwise the statistics would tend to be reversed. If any psychoanalytical principle can be ascribed, it can only be that of Thanatos, the self-destructive death-wish, or perhaps one of masochistic pleasure derived from humiliation or pain. However,

---

17. Joseph Conrad, Three Great Tales (New York: Random House, Inc., 1958), p. 297.
18. Calvin S. Hall & Vernon J. Nordby, The Individual and his Dreams (New York: The New American Library, Inc., 1972), p. 11.

such speculation is both circular and reductive. All one knows is what the subjective consensus has shown. Hall and Nordby stress the negative situations within dreams and proceed further to relate complementary findings on the corresponding aspect of emotions.

> The conclusion is obvious. Many more bad things than good things happen in dreams. This conclusion is highlighted by the results obtained from an analysis of emotions experienced in dreams. The emotions of sadness, anger, apprehension, and confusion are mentioned 565 times in the 1,000 dream reports of young adults. Happy emotions are mentioned only 137 times.[19]

And thus, unpleasant dream emotions outnumber pleasant ones by a factor of over four to one. And therefore both emotional experiences and actual occurrences in dreams, if taken as an indicator of a subconsciously independent force, would imply that the nature of such a force is innately and overtly hostile to man.

Discoveries in sleep research also tend to support this view. Angina, cardiac arrhythmias, nocturnal migraines, duodenal ulcers, and a host of other physical illnesses and ailments undergo further deterioration during REM dreaming.[20] For example, most people who awaken with angina usually awaken directly from a period of REM sleep. Increased gastric acid secretion (discovered in ulcer patients) also occurs only during REM, and not during non-REM sleep. In fact, most illnesses so far monitored during sleep, undergo negative reversals as a consequence of dreams. This fact has led to some speculation among doctors and psychologists that patients who die during the night may very well be dying as a direct result of their dreams. The psychic content and conflict of one's dream may be enough to excite or frighten one literally to death.

Further corroborating evidence comes from the nature of the dream cycle. As the night progresses, REM periods tend to increase in duration, and autonomic functions become more intense. Extensive samplings of psychic dream content also correlate with these physiological facts. Dreams usually become more intense, more

---

19. Ibid., p. 34.
20. Frank R. Freemon, Sleep Research: A Critical Review (Springfield, Illinois: Charles C. Thomas Publishing Company, 1972), pp. 131-132.

bizarre, and generally more active and exciting as the night wears on. During the period just before waking, over half of sleep is devoted to REM dreams. This stressful psychophysical stimulation takes its toll upon the lives of men. For, as any nurse or doctor working night shifts can confirm, the predawn hours just before awakening are known infamously among hospital personnel as the "fatal" ones. Any death, any crisis, usually occurs during the so-called "fatal predawn hours." And so, as consciousness slips further under the malign influence of dreams, the effects are clearly detrimental, if not actively inimical towards man.

Other psychological experiments also augment and support this unsettling view. The theta brain wave pattern (4-7 cycles per second) occurs rarely, if at all, in normal adult waking consciousness. Confined usually to the period as one drifts from light sleep into deep sleep, the slow waves of theta signify the losing of consciousness, the surrendering of will and awareness to the subliminal forces of the mind. Apparently, the only other form in which theta appears during sleep, is in the brief intermittent bursts throughout the process of REM dreaming. Nowhere else during any other level of normal consciousness is theta produced to any significant extent. This exclusively trans-conscious nature of the theta wave pattern has resulted in its unofficial designation as an indicator of contact with the subliminal mind.

The only exception to theta's exclusively REM and transitional, deep sleep nature is its production during profound levels of meditation or trance. Both Zen and yogic practitioners have shown the scientifically demonstrable ability to produce significant amounts of theta during deep meditation. Furthermore, the ability to produce and sustain long trains of uninterrupted theta seems to be proportional to one's development in practiced meditation. Extremely advanced meditators seem able to produce the longest and steadiest, the most abundant quantity and quality of theta brain waves. Whereas less advanced practitioners seem to produce, if at all, only low quality and low quantity trains of theta.

As a result of these empirical observations, an attempt was made to determine the subjective experience of different brain wave patterns and consequently different levels of consciousness and unconsciousness. Experiments by Alyce & Elmer Green at the Menninger Foundation have shown startling results: confirmation of the unpleasant and actively hostile nature of the subliminal mind. Research on Swami Rama, one of the most advanced yogic meditators studied by western scientists, has shown, at least in the Swami's case, a nearly independent force of a definitely negative nature corresponding to the production or release of theta.

> To us, the most interesting of these brain-wave experiments was the last part of item (I.g.): "silencing the conscious mind and bringing forward the subconscious mind." When the Swami did that we observed theta waves in significant amounts in his brain-wave pattern for the first time. When I asked him afterward what that state was like, he said it was unpleasant and noisy. "All of the things that other people wanted me to do, all of the things that I wanted to do, all of the things I should have done but didn't do, came up and began screaming at me at the same time. It is very noisy and very unpleasant. Usually I keep that turned off, but it is useful to look in there once in a while to see what is there.[21]

This statement is impressive because it implies that the subliminal force is of an independent nature. It also shows antagonism that may very well be responsible for mental illness and psychosomatic disease. Corroborating evidence also comes from other sources of medical and psychological research.

Apparently theta, if not in itself representative of a force detrimental to mental health, is at the very least an indication of conflict or discord within man's subconscious mind. In the Synopsis of Electroencephalography, Thomas Barnes summarizes and correlates the information known about theta in the following definition:

> Theta: 5/6 sec. evoked in children by unpleasant stimuli; evoked in adults by termination of pleasant stimulus, (W.G. Walter (1372) EEG J. Sup.) . . . found in psychopathic personalities (A. Hanretta (569) Dis. Nerv. Syst.) . . . significance of theta: frustration.[22]

The implication of both Swami Rama's statement and Barnes' definition is that theta may represent a negative force erupting from

---

21. Elmer & Alyce Green, Beyond Biofeedback (New York: Delacorte Press, 1977), p. 208.
22. Thomas C. Barnes, Synopsis of Electroencephalography or Guide to Brain Waves (New York: Hafner Publishing Company, Inc., 1968), p. 135.

mental conflict and frustration. Whereas Barnes and his colleagues would view theta simply as a result of stress, Swami Rama's experiment implies that this negative tension or disruptive force is actually a causal agent already present. Such provoking stimuli simply makes manifest a force which normally functions within the dormant levels of the mind.

In such a view, theta is indicative of a subliminal force which arises to take hold of consciousness. In a sense, one actually becomes possessed. The dilemma is what comes first, the chicken or the egg? Is theta indicative of an independent force, or is it just a by-product of an abnormal state of mind? In other words, does theta occur as a result of negative thoughts, or is theta, in itself, the force manifesting such thoughts? Whatever the case, both Barnes and the Rama experiment would concur on at least one essential point: theta (the subconscious dream force?) definitely signifies a negative frame of mind.

One point not to be overlooked is that the Green's study appeared nearly a decade after the publication of Barnes' Synopsis. Confronted with such evidence, Barnes may well have supported the independent consciousness hypothesis. In fact, as far as Swami Rama's case is concerned, it seems that theta results from an independent force which causes conflict and frustration. And as was postulated before, this hostile force may be responsible for mental and psychosomatic disease. The theta brain-wave pattern may very well be representative of the malign force after which we seek.

Perhaps this line of reasoning is returning to the unsophisticated, pre-Freudian era when mental disturbance was attributed to an invasion of demons. But simplicity does not necessarily discount the truth. Freud had not the advantage of modern electroencephalographs. His theoretical framework was based solely upon subjective analysis and speculation. Whereas modern psychologists have the benefit of objective methodology, along with a more universal sampling of dream experience and sleep laboratory experiments. As more sophisticated experimental devices collect and correlate an increasing abundance of data, a more coherent and bizarre pattern emerges. The subconscious theta force, whether of a personal or of an alien nature, does appear hostile to man: attacking us every night as we sleep—driving many people to suicide and insanity—crippling and murdering others with sickness and disease—and what is even more frightening—insidiously controlling our lives!

Further evidence correlates slow wave theta and delta (.5 – 3.5 cycles/sec.) with the subliminal force. (It must be noted that delta and theta are very similar in nature, so similar that they are often confused and used interchangeably. Many electro-encephalographers consider the break-off of .5 – 3.5 cps for delta, and 4 – 7 cps for theta, to be a completely arbitrary division not indicative of an actual transition in consciousness. This aspect of sleep stages and cps divisions is debatable, with standards being maintained only out of convenience and conformance. Whatever the case, both theta and delta can be classified as slow waves exclusively indicating the loss of consciousness, or sleep. And delta, the slower, and thus the more severe wave is infamous for its overwhelmingly negative characteristics. Indeed, delta is actually considered by doctors and psychologists as the wave of the three "D's"—disease, destruction, and death!) The malign influence of both theta and delta shows itself in abundance through the negative nature of most slow-wave phenomena.

Pavor nocturnas, the night terror, probably the most traumatic experience known to man (or child) occurs typically between the ages of 4 and 7. Resulting usually during an arousal transition from deep sleep stage 4 to stage 3, the actual psychophysiological attack may very well be an encounter or immersion within the dark forces of the mind. The night terror is characterized and signaled by a K-complex (a violent paroxysmal high-amplitude wave) or a burst of sudden delta activity, investigative eye movements, increased heart and respiratory rate, body movements, and muscular contraction.

Psychologists Kahn, Fisher, and Edwards explain that "The severe Stage 4 night terror consists of perhaps the greatest heart rate acceleration possible in man . . ." [23] The child may suddenly sit up with piercing screams or cries of fear, eyes will be open, and he will appear to be terrified by some experience or vision he often cannot describe. The episode is usually brief but may last up to a half an hour, during which time the victim may moan or talk incoherently, may feel or appear to be choking or suffocating, and will apparently be frightened nearly out of his mind. And what's more, the length of stage 4 before the episode, along with the quantity of delta activity, is directly related to the intensity of the attack.

Apparently the night terror is not the result of a normal dream or nightmare (as would logically be assumed) since the experience takes place during non-REM stages 3 and 4. Also, the usual inability to relate the psychic contents of the experience is the opposite of

---

23. Edwin Kahn, Charles Fisher, & Adele Edwards, "Night Terrors and Anxiety Dreams" in <u>The Mind in Sleep</u> (edited by Arthur M. Arkin, John S. Antrobus, & Steven J. Ellman) (Hillsdale, New Jersey: Lawrence Erlbaum Associates, Inc., Publishers, 1978), p. 533.

awakenings from nightmares. This universal tendency to forget leads psychologists to label the episode as benign. After the night terror, children may smile and return to their normal carefree nature, as though the incident had not even taken place. By morning the child seldom recalls having had the experience.

The fact that even directly following the attack, victims of pavor nocturnas almost never recall their psychic impressions, leads one to assume that some sort of censoring agent is involved. Is it possible that the subliminal force has somehow brainwashed consciousness by overloading the brain and body with intense feelings and sensations? Or is the event so horrible that the conscious mind mercifully blocks out the imagery? One then wonders what might happen when the censors fail, when the experience is not filtered from memory.

In such rare instances the subject may relate either a single vivid image just prior to screaming, or else an elaborate dream sequence following the scream which seems to be related to autonomic activation. According to an experiment on adult subjects by psychologists Kahn, Fisher, and Edwards, "Some of the most severe night terrors involved being crushed or struck by some sudden force, things closing in or being entrapped in a small area, being left alone or abandoned, and choking on or swallowing something . . ."[24] Victims typically describe the feeling of being overwhelmed by some force or condition beyond their control. And thus, the hostile nature of subliminal consciousness seems undeniably confirmed.

There is an abundance of further evidence supporting the notion of an independent consciousness—a consciousness capable of controlling not only man's mind, but also man's body. In order not to belabor the point, a few of the major sleep disturbances will be briefly summarized[*]:

Somnambulism: or sleep-walking, a slow-wave phenomenon occurring during emergence from deep sleep stage 4 to stage 3. When awakened,

---

[*] References for material on sleep disturbances:
   The Mind in Sleep, ibid.
   Sleep Research: A Critical Review, op. cit.
   Sleep and Dreams, Wilse B. Webb & H.W. Agnew, Jr. (Dubuque, Iowa: W.C. Brown Company, 1973).
   EEG of Human Sleep, Robert Leon Williams, Ismet Karacan, & Carolyn J. Hursch (Hoboken, New Jersey: John Wiley & Sons Inc., 1974).

24. Ibid., p. 537.

subjects are bewildered and confused. They have no idea where they were going or what they were doing, and yet subliminal awareness allows them to observe and wander freely, paradoxically conscious and yet unconscious of the surrounding world. Apparently signifies total control and domination of one's conscious mind, will, and body by an obviously unhealthy and completely subliminal force.

Somniloquy: or sleep-talking, once again a slow-wave phenomenon usually occurring during emergence from deep sleep stage 4 to stage 3. When awakened, subjects often cannot recall what they were saying, nor even what they were thinking. Apparently signifies total control over conscious thought processes, perhaps the verbal manifestation of the subconscious.

Bruxism: or teeth-grinding, occurring both during slow-wave deep sleep and also during REM. Apparently indicative of the negative or frustrating nature of both subliminal consciousness and the general unpleasantness of dreams.

If it is true, as it appears, that the force underlying dreaming is inimical to man, then what philosophical stance should one assume? Let us remove ourselves from the realm of concrete psychology and consider the metaphysical ramifications—the meaning and significance of these scientific discoveries. Should we, like Kafka's Joseph K., simply surrender ourselves to the madness and evil? Should we willingly submit to the dark forces within, allowing ourselves to be led like animals to the slaughter? Are we to allow ourselves to be stretched out upon a rock, to let the knife plunge inward, and to die "like a dog?" Is this not what is transpiring as man passively accepts his fate? And yet, what else can one do? Should we, as does Conrad's madman Kurtz, not only recognize and surrender to the underlying horror, but actually affirm it and make it a part of ourselves? If this malevolent force subsumes all existence, then would it not be best to accept it and live it through to the end? Should we not, as does Kurtz, become the quintessential embodiment of such evil—a representative and exemplar of the madness behind life. Or should we, as does Conrad's heroic Marlow, acknowledge the truth of the ultimate "horror", and yet resist it until our last dying breath—with the ascetic discipline of stoic defiance, with the stolid hardness and chilling wisdom of a Prometheus Unbound.

Marlow realizes the dream-like nature of reality, and tries to warn others of the malevolence within the heart of one's subconscious soul—one's "Heart of Darkness". But as Marlow takes note of the dilemma, "It seems to me I am trying to tell you a dream . . ." [25] All his attempts to convey a warning are apparently in vain, for man is a separate and isolated dreamer, totally disconnected from any so-called "common reality." Or as Marlow soon realizes, "No, it is impossible . . .We live, as we dream— alone ...." [26] Nothing in modern literature equals the chilling vision of Conrad's "Heart of Darkness." A man who, by all rights, should have been driven mad—one who has peered over the edge of man's spiritual abyss, returns with only the bleak vision of utter darkness and horror. And so this sojourner and vagabond of the spirit, remains somewhat outside and aloof from human life—a cold, stern judge who knows the somber gravity of the truth.

> Marlow ceased, and sat apart, indistinct and silent, in the pose of a meditating Buddha. Nobody moved for a time.. . . The offing was barred by a black bank of clouds, and the tranquil waterway leading to the uttermost ends of the earth flowed somber under an overcast sky—seemed to lead into the heart of an immense darkness. [27]

And thus, man need not surrender to the "dark truth," but simply acknowledge its validity, and then defy it with all one's strength and will. An intriguing notion is that such defiance will lead to an out-and-out battle of consciousness: Subliminal vs. the Conscious Mind. Such an idea is presented in Colin Wilson's science-fiction novel, The Mind Parasites.

The story's plot is of alien entities residing within the depths of the unconscious mind. Leeching the flow of energy available to consciousness, it is because of these parasites that man can utilize only a few percent of his brain power, for the remaining mental energy has been greedily siphoned off. Apparently these subliminal beings release only the bare minimum of energy necessary for their hosts'

25. Conrad, op. cit., p. 246.
26. Conrad, op. cit., p. 246.
27. Conrad, op. cit., p. 307.

survival.

The story continues with a group of scientists discovering the presence of these entities and consequently committing suicide or being driven insane. Only the heroic narrator, along with a few other "stronger spirits," manage to descend into their unconscious, confront with mental combat, and eventually drive these hostile forces literally out of their minds. The result is a sudden flow of unimpeded energy as the parasites are wiped forever from human consciousness. These completely "free" minds suddenly gain godlike powers of awareness and control. They represent the new race of supermen into which mankind will evolve.

A much more intriguing novel by Colin Wilson is The Philosophers' Stone. The plot of the story is of two scientists' descent into the depths of consciousness. The result is a frightening encounter with subliminal forces which, stirred momentarily from dormancy, briefly manifest themselves in the scientists' everyday lives. At first these forces appear to be demonic, but as the experimenters tap the flow of unconscious energy, the understanding dawns that this is only a subjectively-biased view. In reality these hidden forces are of a godlike nature, so far above man, as man is above insects. If these dormant "gods" residing on a subliminal plane of awareness just happen to awaken, the violent upheaval of power will mark the end of the human race. For just as man takes no notice of the ants he crushes, neither will these proto-gods notice the trivial world of human life. The conclusion of these scientists is that man must increase and accelerate his normal conscious evolution, raising himself, if not to the level of these subliminal gods, then at least to the level where he will be recognized as a clearly intelligent and evolving conscious life form.

The Philosophers' Stone:
Dreams as the Looking Glass of Life

The Philosophers' Stone seems to suggest that the apparent negativity of the subconscious force may be the result, not of an observational error, but rather the result of an interpretive one. A man treading upon a bug is not consciously hostile, but to the ants he would undoubtedly be considered malign. Even in the case of conscious knowledge of actions, the situation is not as clear-cut as it would seem. A child playing beside an anthill stomping upon ants, could not really be considered evil. But this is only because of our understanding of the child. To both child and man, ants are of no consequence, and so the child's aggressive tendencies are held to be merely recreation or fun. But to the ants, the child and all humanity could reasonably be viewed as purely demonic—a force to be contended with and if possible destroyed. And such may indeed be the relation between man's conscious and subconscious—a morass of misunderstanding and confusion. Could the force within or beyond the subliminal realm, in reality be totally indifferent to man? Could all conflict, all frustration, all confusion and anxiety be simply the result of contact with an uncontrolled power? If it is true that the force is indifferent to man, then one should presumably find not just exclusively negative results. A discrepancy should arise within experiments and observations, perhaps not enough to offset general tendencies and conclusions, but a discrepancy that remains inexplicable nevertheless. And this is apparently just the case.

According to Hall and Nordby, dreams of misfortune far outnumber dreams of good fortune. But if dreams are characteristic of the subconscious, then why is there this dual or Janus-faced nature? If the dream force is indeed out to "get us," then every dream should accordingly be unpleasant. But they aren't. In fact most dreams are mundane, thus supporting the hypothetically indifferent nature of the subliminal force.* It is only of those dream experiences which are classifiable as either good or bad, that the negative far outnumber the reports of the positive. Hall and Nordby consider this to be the result of a subjective preprogramming phenomenon. Man, whether modern cosmopolitan or primitive aborigine, views the world as generally a hostile place. And thus, all inner tension is simply integrated, affirmed, and reflected through dreams. The fact that joyous and pleasant dreams even occur, tends to confirm the theory that dreams have no absolute nature, but rather are a result of purely subjective experience.

Other psychological theories and observations not only contradict the negative nature of the subconscious, but allows for the possibility of a benign agency or force. Although delta waves are labeled with the signification of the three "D's"—disease, destruction, and death; many doctors and psychologists advocate a fourth, positive "D"—that delta is perhaps an agency of "defense."

Imagine how it would be if, after a severe accident, one remained in either a conscious or semi-conscious state, suffering hour after hour of prolonged agonizing pain. The ability of the mind and body to enter the delta state of coma is perhaps the most merciful unconscious instinct ever devised. For during coma the mind is spared all pain and suffering, and the body is generally deactivated in order to repair damage. Thus the "D" of defense is an anomaly in the negativistic theory of the subliminal mind. In fact, this defense mechanism of delta is the most pronounced objection to such a theory, capable in itself of refuting such an interpretation. For if the subconscious is actually inimical to man, then would it not be in its interests to allow one to experience pain?—to suffer through the torments of a living hell? The "D" of defense contradicts any view of subconscious malevolence.

Another discrepancy is the dual nature of theta. While theta waves signify the presence of negative thoughts and feelings, they also paradoxically signify euphoria, creativity, and enlightened tranquility. This evidence comes from investigations of both biofeedback training and also the previously mentioned research on Zen and yogic meditation. And while Swami Rama is one of the most advanced meditators studied by western scientists, his subjective experience of

---

* *This evidence comes from sleep-lab experiments in which subjects were awakened during REM in order to relate their dreams. Whereas Hall and Nordby collected data by means of questionnaires, questionnaires that were distributed to be filled out at leisure in the subject's own homes. Hence it is fair to conclude that only the more vivid and exciting dreams were usually remembered and reported.*

the theta pattern does not correspond with those of other advanced disciples of either Zen or yoga. Such meditators and biofeedback subjects relate a feeling of euphoria, of profound relaxation, of well-being and tranquility. Zen masters are said to have transcended normal consciousness—their awareness passing into a mystical realm of "knowing" rather than "thinking." On the other hand, unlike this feeling of satori or the active hostility "within" Swami Rama, many biofeedback subjects and meditators relate an entirely different experience of hypnagogic hallucinations and dream-like sequences accompanying theta. This multi-faceted aspect of the theta wave pattern lends credence to the subjective theory of the subconscious. This is further corroborated by the paradoxical, destructive-creative physiological processes accompanying dreams.

This additional discrepancy in the malevolence theory shows that, although generally the subconscious leans overwhelmingly towards the malign, there are still many cases where it seems to foster man's inner growth. There is no need to belabor these positive, dynamic aspects of the subconscious, for they are the well-known province of popular psychology and the occult-mystical market.

Briefly summarized, the subconscious has shown a remarkable ability to retain and correlate both knowledge and wisdom. Throughout history dreams have played an important role in determining man's future through visions and prophecies, through flashes of insight, through creative inspiration which guided and enhanced man's understanding. Such stories are replete within folklore, religion, and throughout the body of dream literature. And so, while dreams often appear definitely "bad," one must not forget that, in many cases, they also appear definitely "good." While in other instances they appear to be neutral—as random, disjointed, and as meaningless as life. This evidence indicates that dreams are simply a subjective phenomena, perhaps as imbued with meaning or the lack of meaning as is each individual's subjective life.

The possibility exists that through dreams and the subconscious one may be tapping the transconscious reality behind existence—Alice's sleeping Red King beyond the "Looking-Glass." This entity sleeping within the chess-dream of life may be a vast powerhouse, a dynamo of creative-destruction, the central piece vital to the continued flow of the game. Is it possible that this subconscious force is as indifferent to man as is Wilson's dormant gods? Could this anonymous, perhaps independent force be a focal point, a conductor or generator of the underlying reality? Is this the explanation for such diverse experiences of subliminal contact—this Janus-faced nature of the subconscious realm? Could this unconscious or perhaps consciously indifferent force be open to indiscriminate contact from man? Could its paradoxical manifestations result from allowing anyone, whether advanced or degenerate, to draw freely upon its reservoirs for any purpose or non-purpose under the sun. And thus, this unexclusive liberal nature results in effects both positive and negative, good and evil, creative and even self-destructive. Could the tendency toward negativism be only a statistical display of man's flawed imperfection? In other words, is it simply man's foolhardiness that he employs this limitless power for self-punishment and doom? Is mankind's present situation comparable to a child playing with matches who inadvertently scorches his fingers and even burns down his own house?

If this is true, then man could be his own worst enemy, literally the cause of all his troubles and fears. Tapping the inner power source would consequently animate his paranoia, his guilt and frustration, his anxiety, spiritual conflict, mental illness and disease. Man himself could be the source of his own subliminal discord and distress, programming his psyche for a nightmare journey into madness, suffering, and ultimately Conrad's "The Horror!"

The Dream of Life

"Is all our Life, then, but a dream..." [28]

Lewis Carroll

The question is whether this dream-world analogy could possibly be true of life itself. Could man not only be responsible for his subjective inner world of dreams, but also for his subjective outer world of reality? Could man be responsible for creating his own life, for developing and accepting, just as in dreams, his own conscious reality—his own pattern of life? Is this what Aldous Huxley meant when he dictated from his deathbed in the last essay of his life: "The world is an illusion, but it is an illusion which we must take seriously . . ." [29]

The problem is not one of true reality or illusion, for this itself is unimportant. What is important is what we choose to be real, or rather the psychic and spiritual effect such impressions make upon our mind, our being, and consequently upon our own world, our own soul. Perhaps this is the message behind dreams—that reality is valid only within the domain of the mind, that thoughts and ideas, or in other words "dreams," are the closest approximation of the absolute truth. Or as Anatole France explains in The Revolt of the Angels: "This shape is real, because it is apparent, and all the realities in the world are but appearances." [30]

28. Lewis Carroll, Sylvie and Bruno (from The Complete Illustrated Lewis Carroll), (New York: W.H. Smith Publishers Inc., 1991), p.253.
29. Aldous Huxley from "Shakespeare and Religion" in Aldous Huxley: Complete Essays (Chicago: Ivan R. Dee, Publisher, 2002), Volume VI, p. 159.
30. Anatole France, The Revolt of the Angels (New York: The Heritage Press, 1953), p. 64.

The possibility stands metaphysically unchallenged, that all existence may be nothing more than appearance. And so once again we are back to square one. As the first proto-man awoke from a strange, perhaps terrifying dream, he poses the ultimate philosophical question: "Was it real?" And consequently, "What in fact is real?" Are dreams unreal simply because they appear elusive and ever-changing? Should waking life be considered real simply because it appears stable and consistent? But just as all dream-reality vanishes as one awakens to waking life, so too perhaps all life-reality vanishes as one awakens to the Ultimate Dream.

Could it be that both dreams and life are of the same undifferentiated substance, the same confusing mixture of reality and illusion? The only difference may merely be one of cohesive "appearance" and duration. Even Albert Einstein (a stalwart advocate of a realistic universe) maintains: "Reality is merely an illusion, albeit a very persistent one." [31] Hence, life may be nothing more than an unusually long dream which will culminate as one awakens through death. If this is true—if this has even the slightest semblance of truth, then mankind is in for the supreme "rude awakening." Or as Hermann Hesse writes in the final pages of his last novel:

> Suddenly the long years he had lived, the treasures cherished, the delights enjoyed, the pangs suffered, the fears endured, the despair he had tasted to the brink of death—all this had been taken from him, extinguished, reduced to nothingness. And yet not to nothingness! For the memory was there. The images had remained with him. . . .
>
> ...All that crowded reality had been a dream. Perhaps, too, he had dreamed all that had happened previously... And was what he was experiencing this moment, what he saw before his eyes...together with what he was now thinking about it all—was not all this made of the same stuff? Was it not dream, illusion, Maya? And everything he would still experience in the future, would see with his eyes and feel with his hands, up to the moment of his death—was it any different in substance, any different in kind? It was all a game and a sham, all foam and dream. It

---

31. Albert Einstein from a speech to the New History Society, December 14, 1930 as quoted by David Michie, Buddhism for Busy People (Ithaca, New York: Snow Lion Publications, 2008), p. 175.

was Maya, the whole lovely and frightful, delicious and desperate kaleidoscope of life with its searing delights, its searing griefs.

He had had enough and more than enough of this dreaming, of this diabolic texture of experiences, joys, and sufferings that crushed your heart and made your blood stand still, only to be suddenly revealed as Maya, so that you were nothing but a fool. He had had enough of everything. He no longer craved either wife or child, either a throne or victory or revenge, either happiness or cleverness, either power or virtue. He desired nothing but peace, nothing but an end of turmoil. He no longer wanted anything but to check this endlessly turning wheel, to stop this endless spectacle, to extinguish it all... [32]

And so Dasa, the hero and narrator of the story, rejects the world of human life. Experiencing through a vivid dream the quintessential illusion of life, he conversely realizes that life is nothing more than a dream, simply an illusion, though not a "simple" illusion, but rather Maya, the paradoxical real illusion. Thus Dasa abandons humanity as he learns the parable of the Ultimate Dream. His own life is unimportant. For his energy is now dedicated towards the transcendent realm—Through the Looking-Glass and beyond the confusing chess-dream of Life. The last words of The Glass Bead Game, the last real words of Hermann Hesse's literary life: "There is no more to be told about Dasa's life, for all the rest took place in a realm beyond pictures and stories. He never again left the forest." [33] And neither did Hesse. Almost as a prophetic summary of his life, Hesse turned inward during the remainder of his old age becoming somewhat of a kindly hermit, secluded from humanity in his ivory-tower mountain retreat.

Thomas Mann relates how, after traveling all the way from England, he happened to be in the area of Hesse's home in Switzerland, went out of his way, traveled for hours up to his secluded mountain retreat, only to find a sign on the front gate of Hesse's home—a sign which related a Chinese proverb of how a man in his old age has earned the right to live the rest of life undisturbed and in peace. Mann acceded

---

32. Hermann Hesse, The Glass Bead Game (New York: Holt, Rhinehart and Winston, Inc., 1969), pp. 555-556.
33. Ibid., p. 558.

to Hesse's wishes and left Switzerland without paying his intended visit. Thomas Mann and Hermann Hesse never again saw one another alive . . .

And so, it may well be that dreams and reality are intertwined within one paradoxically real unreality. In such a case, dreams may actually serve as a catalyst in revealing to man the strange dream of life. And thus both Dasa and Hesse, realizing the transient unreality of life, retire inward to find solace within the only reality—the ultimate reality of one's inner self.

This transcendental dream nature would imply a transcendental dream consciousness. Perhaps the force behind dreams is then somehow beneficial to man. One could justify an indifferent dream nature, and even to some extent one of active malevolence, but with all the discrepancies, both good, bad and neutral, could one support a view of subliminal benevolence—a force actively working to improve man's lot? With all the conflicting data is there any interpretation which could explain this view? The question involves the very nature of man and what is defined as, in the long run, "beneficial." If man's present state of awareness is the apex of evolution—the culmination of mental and spiritual development—then obviously any threat, conflict, or interference can be designated as inimical or bad.

But is this man's current status? If not—if there is any chance that this proposition is false, then it is possible, perhaps probable, that this dream force may be attempting to aid mankind—transforming him to a higher level of consciousness, opening the doorway to a transcendental realm. And just as Dasa, after his disillusionment, wanted to destroy the world, so too perhaps all negative aspects of the subconscious result from the fear of transcendence—resistance to the revelation that one's life is nothing more than a dream. Such a fear would be a fear of the transcendental unknown, but much more intensely a fear of abandoning or losing one's reality, one's sense of being, one's illusions—one's life.

But what if there is no transcendental realm? What if the Red King awakens to a dream within a dream? What if all of life is simply a dream, an illusion, everything that exists being merely the elusive images of an eternally-dreaming mind. What if everything in the end boils down to nothing—nothing but the haunting emptiness of Twain's "illusions of life"? What if Satan was right?—that nothing exists but empty dreams, foolish dreams, grotesque dreams. What then could one do? Destroy the world? Destroy oneself? Destroying everything would make no difference, for the force of illusion is not only operating through us, but operating throughout and beyond all space and time. It is an inherent, metaphysical structure of being—as long as any possibility or any thought exists, so too will exist the real illusion.

And so one is lost forever within the labyrinthine world of endless dreams, unable to escape to any transcendental sanctuary, unable to escape to Hesse's visionary realm of peace, for all such realms are merely childish delusions. And so, like Thomas Mann we return home to England, sadly rejected through the tragic necessity of Fate.

But is this not the easy way out? Must man forever be told what is good and what is bad, what is true and what is false, how to live—how to dream? Must the enigma of dream-reality be seen as indicting and berating life as nothing more than a dream, or can it be viewed from the more awesome perspective that dreams are no less real than life. As was stated before, dreams may in fact be a valid conscious experience, as real, perhaps more real than anything else in one's life.

Could this be the key to understanding dreams: that consciousness creates its own reality, that reality is only real within the domain of the mind? Perhaps the nightmare behind both dreams and life is the nightmare we ourselves both create and accept. Dreams and life may ultimately be unreal, but the impression they make upon our mind and our being is a haven which may last until the end of time. And thus, in a world where everything has become a dream, dreams consequently become the only reality. One must then accept dreams for what they are, eventually learning to become the best possible dreamer—the Ultimate Dreamer transcending both dreams and life. Or as Satan explains in The Mysterious Stranger: "But I, your poor servant, have revealed you to yourself and set you free. Dream other dreams, and better!" [34]

Perhaps the best expression of this enlightened resolve is the obscure, anonymous novel The Endless Dream. The story is a quest for the meaning and purpose of life. It is a spiritual odyssey of the soul, revealing one man's search and ultimate confrontation with the truth. The journey is made via the surrealistic imagery of dreams and illusions. The narrator and hero of the story presses onward through life, penetrating to the very depths of his soul. In his metaphysical encounter with reality he realizes that life is only a dream, a passing phantom that would soon be gone. Life was an illusion. The world was an illusion. There was no reality but the reality of illusions. The sudden revelation transforms the world. In a flash the scene fades as he finds himself, once more, at the beginning of the story. The entire

34. Twain, op. cit., p. 252.

journey was a figment of his mind. The vision leaves him in a state of apathy and despair.

> Aimlessly wandering, I drift through the world. Void of purpose and soul, I no longer seek. Forgetful of all former dreams, indifferent to all future life, I die a thousand times too late. And in the end I don't complain. I let it pass before my eyes—the pain, the useless suffering, endurance of appointed roles. I wander through an endless dream, specter in an empty scene where nothing more is being shown.[35]

But in the end he discovers that there is something more to life; that through defiance and endurance lies a vision of hope; that the spirit can create its own dream, and the soul its own destiny. In a strangely haunting book of dreams he discovers a sense of meaning and purpose. The novel ends with the concluding lines of a story within a story.

> He listened to the dead silence, the empty stillness of a frozen, stagnant world. Unconcerned and unaware, the world slept peacefully through the night. He was disillusioned and about to turn back when suddenly his feet reached the snowy path. The light, powdered snow crunched under his boots, echoing footsteps through the tall, pine trees. The sound in the soundless, the heartbeat of perfection, filled his body with courage and strength. The footsteps resounded through the hidden world like the regimental march of a one-man army. Half asleep, dazed by the illusion of life, his soul wandered back and lingered in the bright, crystal cavern of his dream.[36]

---

35. Anonymous (edited by Wayne Omura), <u>The Endless Dream</u>, unpublished manuscript.
36. <u>Ibid.</u>

PART TWO

The Dream of a Reality

"We are such stuff as dreams are made on;
And our little life is rounded with a sleep." [37]

— *William Shakespeare*

37. William Shakespeare, <u>The Tempest</u> (Baltimore, Maryland: Penguin Books Inc., 1968), p. 120.

Dream and Reality

"All that we see or seem is but a dream within a dream." [38]

— *Edgar Allan Poe*

The dream exists. It is phenomenally real. It is the source of creativity and madness. The subject of Part Two is not whether dreams are objectively real, for such speculation is open to endless debate. Rather, what is considered is the possible effect such dreams (whether real or illusory) have upon structuring reality. Metaphysically speaking, life itself may be considered one long dream, for all one knows is subjective experience, and such subjectivity may indeed be false. The objective world (if it does in fact exist) can never be known, for the mind and body, along with universal physical laws, effectively filter perception and thus alter experience. Consciousness is therefore enclosed within a subjective universe. The terms "real" and "unreal," "objective" and "subjective" lose all meaning, for everything is of the same undifferentiated substance.

All that can be known derives from all that one perceives. Perception is thus the criterion for determining reality. Havelock Ellis's pronouncement that "Dreams are true while they last. Can we, at the best, say more of life?" [39] is hence profound in its implication of the all-encompassing parameter of subjectivity. Dreams may not be objectively real, but then neither may be the experiences of life. Chuang Tzu's butterfly dilemma can never be resolved.

---

38. Edgar Allan Poe, "A Dream within a Dream" from <u>Edgar Allan Poe: Selected Prose, Poetry, and Eureka</u> (San Francisco: Rhinehart Press, ?), p. 482.
39. Ellis, <u>op. cit.</u>, p. 281.

> Once upon a time, I, Chuang Tzu, dreamt I was a butterfly, fluttering hither and thither, to all intents and purposes a butterfly. I was conscious only of following my fancies as a butterfly, and was unconscious of my individuality as a man. Suddenly, I awaked, and there I lay, myself again. Now I do not know whether I was then a man dreaming I was a butterfly, or whether I am now a butterfly, dreaming I am a man.[40]

A foolproof argument cannot be sustained, for all that is known is the perceiving consciousness. Chuang Tzu could be a butterfly or a man. One can never know. But within a subjective universe it doesn't matter. Chuang Tzu, the butterfly, experiences. Chuang Tzu, the man, experiences. Dream or reality, they are subjectively the same. There is no difference to Chuang Tzu's consciousness. Hence the validity of so-called "imaginary" dreams.

The dream is itself (whether metaphysically real or illusory) a valid realm of subjective experience. This is the solution to the dream-reality dilemma proposed by the Spanish writer Pedro Calderón de la Barca. In his play Life is a Dream a potential heir to the throne finds himself the victim of a conspiracy. Taken prisoner and drugged, he is tricked into believing that his former experiences were a dream. He thus vacillates in his convictions between dreams, false realities, and the nightmare of his real life until he regains his rightful throne and restores order to his kingdom.

However his confusing states of consciousness have left their toll. Bewildered by the contradictory versions of his subjective reality, Segismundo begins to wonder whether or not he is still dreaming. Is he the ruler of his kingdom or will he once again awaken to find himself a prisoner in a dungeon? Realizing the incontrovertible logic of this reasoning, Segismundo ends Calderón's play by maintaining that one can never really know whether one is experiencing reality or a dream, and thus the most that can be done is to live and experience one's perceptions "as though" they were real. One is responsible for oneself and one's actions whether within a dream or within waking life—the validity of subjective reality remaining for both essentially the same. Segismundo's character is hence transformed through his acceptance of this metaphysical limbo of uncertainty:

---

40. Herbert A. Giles, Chuang Tzu: Taoist Philosopher and Chinese Mystic (London: George Allen & Unwin, Ltd., 1926), p. 47.

Basilio: Thy wisdom is a marvel to us all.
Astolfo: And what a change his nature now reveals!
Rosaura: And how discreet and prudent he's become!
Segismundo: What is it that surprises all of you?
What startles you, if my perceptor was
A dream, and in anxiety I fear
I shall awake and find myself again
Imprisoned? Even though this were not so,
It is sufficient just to dream it is.
For this is how I learned, so it would seem,
That all our mortal bliss fades like a dream.[41]

The instability of normal reality, the nightmare of Segismundo's life, can thus serve as a catalyst in undermining the "absolute" structure of existence. Segismundo can never know for certain whether his bliss or his misfortune are "really" real, and thus it is sufficient that he simply believes them to be. And yet this undifferentiated approach, while philosophically sound, nevertheless lends an illusory quality to human existence. Hence the reason for Calderón's title: Life _is_ a Dream.*

---

*_Italics mine._

41. Pedro Calderón de la Barca, Life is a Dream (Woodbury, New York: Barron's Educational Series, Inc., 1958), p. 101.

SECTION ONE

The Classical Approach

"Thus shall you think of all this fleeting world:
A star at dawn, a bubble in a stream;
A flash of lightning in a summer cloud.
A phantom, an illusion, a dream." [42]

— *Buddha*

42. Buddha, <u>The Diamond Sutra</u>, Chapter XXXII.

Phenomenalism:
Life as an Impression?

*"For, try as we may, we cannot get behind the ap-
pearance of things to the reality. And the terrible
reason may be that there is no reality in things
apart from their appearances."* [43]

— *Oscar Wilde*

Calderón, Wilde, and even the Buddha seem to be suggesting that
life is tantamount to a dream. But is it? Is life actually one long dream?
According to phenomenalism, life may indeed be simply a dream, for
all that exists are sensory impressions or "sensa." Phenomenalism
maintains that all that can be experienced is the world of phenomena,
and that there is <u>no</u> existence apart from the phenomenal. Objective
reality in itself does not exist unless simply as groups or series
of sensa. Thus the world is a subjective impression of the mind, a
tentative world where objects cease existing the moment they are
no longer perceived. The hypothetical tree falling in the forest is
brought literally "to mind," for phenomenalistically speaking such an
unwitnessed event would make no sound. Hence, reality is defined by
the subjective interaction with the senses—mental perception being
the sole criterion for determining what is real.

The phenomenalistic argument is valid on the simplistic level, i.e.
one perceives the light from the sun and not the sun itself. In such
a case it is obvious that the "real" objective sun can never be known,
but only the secondhand world of its sensory impressions. Objective
reality as such does not exist. The sun does not, in and of itself, exist,

---

43. Hesketh Pearson, <u>Oscar Wilde: His Life and Wit</u> (New York: Harper &
Brothers, Publishers, 1946), p. 186.

but only in and through and by virtue of its light.

The objective sun, however, cannot be obliterated so easily. Its ghostly presence lingers to haunt the argument of subjectively "real" light. For with only sensa to go by there is no basis in tangible reality—all criteria returning to the subjective mind. Reality is hence tantamount to a strange dream where feelings and effects float about without a knowable cause. The standard of reference is lost and therefore the sense of reality. All that one knows is the fading impressions of a dream.

The metaphysical painter Giorgio de Chirico projects phenomenalistic theory into the realm of art. Basing his creations on the premise that the world consists solely of appearances or phenomena, Chirico's expressions take the form of a tentative dream. An ambiguous tension permeates the atmosphere of his uncanny paintings, a feeling that something ominous is about to occur, or that something momentous has just taken place. It is an elusive atmosphere which has no cause, no apparent reason for creating its effect. Vague figures without substance are frozen in eternal suspense. Hidden nooks and darkened corridors extend beyond the painting's limits. Facades stand isolated amidst a vast, desolate plain. The long shadows of sunset warp the landscape with the ambiguity of a dream. The world, as phenomenalistically expressed in the metaphysical artwork of Chirico, exhibits the uncertainty of a reality exclusively defined by sensa. Chirico verbalizes his doubts in a statement concerning one of his paintings.

> Could life be but an immense lie? Could it be the
> shadow of a fleeting dream? Could it be but the echo
> of mysterious rappings struck over there on the rocks
> of the mountain, whose opposite side, it seems, no
> one has ever seen.[44]

It is the phenomenalistic fallacy. For if reality is simply the perception or assimilation of sensa, then something is obviously awry with the universal order. For how could sensory stimuli exist without a cause? How could sunlight possibly exist without an objectively real sun? Phenomenalism thus renders life a mere play of shadows—a world of sensations without causal substance. There are no noumena

---

44. Giorgio de Chirico, <u>De Chirico by de Chirico</u> (New York: The New York Cultural Center, 1972), p. 97.

(things in themselves), but only phenomena. Life is hence tantamount to a whimsical dream. But what if one takes a more refined approach?

Giorgio de Chirico. *Melancholy and Mystery of a Street.* 1914

Giorgio de Chirico. *The Joys and Enigmas of a Strange Hour.* 1913

Representative Realism

According to the philosophy of representative realism, the objective world exists in and of itself and manifests its presence through sensory stimuli or sensa. Thus the sun is an objectively real noumenon ("thing-in-itself") which manifests its reality through the medium of its light. Hence light, or subjectively perceived sensations, are not the essence of reality, but simply its mode of conveyance. The objective world exists, manifesting itself through its corresponding sensa. The unreality of phenomenalism is thus surmounted with a reappraisal of objective manifestation. This more "realistic" approach is the very basis of common sense and logic regardless of whether it is acknowledged as such. The world is considered as consisting of material objects which continue to exist whether or not they are perceived. The premise is the foundation of science, technology, and normal everyday life. Objective reality exists independent of the perceiver and is not some inexplicable, phenomenalistic "dream." And yet the limitations of space-time emerge to literally warp representative realism's "vision" of reality.

The amazing school-day facts of astronomy return to haunt the mind. The light from the sun takes approximately eight minutes to reach earth. During that interval the sun could have gone nova, and yet the earth and its inhabitants would be unaware of the catastrophe. Nothing can travel faster than the speed of light, and thus the world would be ignorant of its impending doom. In effect as one looks at the sun one is actually looking at the past. One is seeing the reality of the sun as it was eight minutes earlier. The problem is magnified the farther one looks into space.

Andromeda, the closest comparable galaxy to the Milky Way, is not only 2.5 million light years in distance, but also 2.5 million years in the past. At the farthest reaches of the visible universe a strange object known as quasar (ULAS J1120 + 0641) is   separated by 12.9 billion years of time. It is 12.9 billion light years distant, and yet it radiates the energy of 63 trillion stars. Our Milky Way galaxy is composed of approximately 300 billion stars. This one object is emitting the equivalent of 210 Milky Ways! But does it still exist in the present, 12.9 billion years later?

This remote quasar is the best known example of how distance and time can alter our view of what we take for reality. At a certain point, what actually exists as opposed to what appears to exist 12.9 billion years ago is so different that you may as well be viewing an illusion. For what is an illusion, after all, but an appearance or projection which doesn't correspond to reality? So much time has elapsed that cosmologists believe this quasar, as it appears 12.9 billion years in the past, no longer exists in the same form. It eventually evolved by either being swallowed up in a super-massive black hole; ejecting its mass in far-flung plasma streams into distant space; or even re-condensing into nebulae, stars, and galaxies-- the rest of the familiar, known universe (closer to home, literally. Perhaps even into something similar to ourselves and our surroundings.) The paradox is: how could we be viewing a bizarre reality which may now have become our current reality? Is light a time-portal into the past? Are we, in some way, observing a ghostly illusion?

Whereas the basic premise of phenomenalism is that objective reality (in the form of noumena) does not exist, the realistic argument, by granting a common-sense approach to reality, results in a consequent distortion of reality. At the very least, the realistic view leads to a delayed reality. But which is in fact worse, the ghostly reality of phenomenalism or the delayed and distorted reality of concrete realistic thought?

The physical disparity increases on the macrocosmic scale to the point where astronomical observations can no longer be trusted, for the finite speed limit of light inherently distorts perception. The fact that reality cannot be communicated instantaneously but must, by physical necessity, be conveyed through a sensory medium results in an unavoidable misconception of the world. Reality itself is never actually present but rather, by physical limitations, always past. Regardless of how close or how far the object of perception the very nature of separation separates the present from the past.

One can therefore only know the reality of the past—a reality which by definition no longer exists. Hence, one can only know misrepresentations of existence, past realities such as quasars, real illusions such as life. The present moment can never be known, for the external world must translate itself into subjective experience, and this translation necessarily requires time. Thus all that can be perceived are real illusions—real in the sense that this is all one can know, illusions in the sense that the object of the manifestation no longer exists as the same.

The paradox of representative realism's delayed reality is borne out in Franz Kafka's story "The Great Wall of China." In this metaphysical analogue of the cosmos Kafka illustrates the "astronomical" problems of modern science and its consequent effect upon one's vision of reality and meaning.

The story relates how the Emperor of China issues forth decrees to the people of his vast, cosmic empire. The messengers must cross immense distances in order to reach the isolated outlying provinces. The journey takes years to accomplish: "So vast is our land that no fable could do justice to its vastness, the heavens can scarcely span it—."[45] The arrival is seen to be absurd and ironic, for the villagers adhere to customs and decrees, a world and a reality long since past. The dynasty has changed again and again. The emperor they revered has passed away in bygone ages few can remember.

The comical absurdity of living in a past reality alters the villagers' entire outlook on life. For why obey these "new" laws and decrees when the interval of delivery has already made them antiquated and out-of-date? The messenger's journey, rather than enlightening, has also conveyed a non-existent reality. The mistrust engendered by the requisite factor of time, results in a denial of all so-called reality, even that reality which is by comparison relatively present. A revolt breaks out in a neighboring province. A beggar appears with a leaflet, presumably to enlist aid. Yet he is laughed at and driven out of the room. The reason?

> ...certain turns of the written word, which for us have an archaic character. Hardly had the priest read two pages before we had come to our decision. Ancient history told long ago, old sorrows long since healed. And though—so it seems to me in recollection—the gruesomeness of the living present was irrefutably conveyed by the beggar's words, we laughed and

---

45. Franz Kafka, The Great Wall of China: Stories and Reflections (New York: Schocken Books Inc., 1946), p. 92.

shook our heads and refused to listen any longer. So eager are our people to obliterate the present.

If from such appearances anyone should draw the conclusion that in reality we have no Emperor, he would not be far from the truth.[46]

Indeed, for the past itself no longer exists and the present moment can only be conveyed through time. A delayed reality is thus illusory by nature, being a past, nonexistent reality which is, to all effects, equivalent to no reality. Hence the villagers' understandable eagerness to "obliterate the present," for regardless of how close, the present is, by physical limitations, only apparent. It does not exist to the subjective perceiver, for it is to him always past. The Emperor may just as well not exist, for by the time his reality becomes manifest it is no longer real. Hence the Emperor is, to his people, simply an illusion—an illusion whose commandments cannot be believed or obeyed.

The realistic approach of modern thought is thus even more unstable than the "sensational" premise of phenomenalism. For with phenomenalism external reality is only phenomena, totally unknowable and nonexistent as noumena. Whereas the logic of realism, while acknowledging the knowableness of objective reality, leads inevitably to distortion and the eventual dissipation of reality. With realism the "appearance" is treated as though real—an approach practically sound, but leading to complications on both cosmic and metaphysical levels of perception. It must be remembered that this perceptual dilemma of gauging reality is not confined to metaphysics and epistemology, but has a tangible basis in observable fact.

Cosmologists must contend with the problems of space and time as they observe and analyze a universe 13.7 billion years in the past. Is this reality or illusion? The universe 13.7 billion light-years away in space was radically different from the universe as it "appears" at present. The world assumes paradoxical characteristics as astrophysicists become tentative about the nature of the reality they are observing. Proponents of the Cosmic Inflation Theory such as Alan Guth believe the very laws of physics were different near the "Big Bang." (The four fundamental forces were merged into one force. At one point, gravity did not attract, it instead repulsed—or rather, the one force repulsed. Areas of the universal expansion took place faster-than-light.)

---

46. Ibid., p. 96.

An even more bizarre alternative to Cosmic Inflation is the Cyclic Model of String/M Theory. It, too, acknowledges the breakdown of the fundamental laws of physics at the cosmic singularity known as the Big Bang. But it opens the universe into eleven dimensions rather than the known four. And it goes back in time before the Big Bang. String theorists Paul Steinhardt and Neil Turok propose that collisions of parallel, extra-dimensional string membranes created the Big Bang. There was no true beginning. These collisions occur endlessly resulting in a continual cycle of Big Bangs.

Cosmologists are theorizing about conditions so far distant in space and time that different physical laws apply and extra dimensions may come into play. The universe near the Big Bang obviously no longer exists in the same form. It is alien to how it appears at present. The early universe is only an image projected from the past—a past which is itself presently an illusion.

Thus the premise of representative realism, if correct, makes the world an uncanny place in which to live. For present objective reality is so far distant that it can never be known. It is separated by a gulf which can never be bridged. Kafka is therefore justified in commenting: "If from such appearances anyone should draw the conclusion that in reality we have no Emperor, he would not be far from the truth."[47] For an intangible past is irrelevant to the present. Furthermore, while representative realism acknowledges the noumena which phenomenalism denies, it nevertheless brings the perceiver no closer to their essence. The noumena are left suspended in a metaphysical void. The realistic premise, as with phenomenalism, still holds phenomena as the primary conveyor of reality. Thus the world, in itself, is an unobserved and unintelligible causal factor of perception—all that the subjective mind perceives being merely a world of phenomena or effects. Hence the theory, though practical on the common-sense level, breaks down when extended to the level of the cosmos. Representative realism is thus inadequate in coping with the real reality of life, for according to its implications, just as with the Emperor, the universe as it appears cannot be believed. Therefore reality, as depicted by Kafka and representative realism, is analogous to a frustrating dream beyond hope of comprehension.

In the parable of "An Imperial Message" Kafka dramatizes the dilemma realism poses for mankind. The Emperor on his deathbed sends a message to you, "his humble subject, the insignificant shadow

---

47. Ibid., p. 96.

cowering in the remotest distance before the imperial sun."[48] The messenger, strong and unyielding, fights his way through the throngs of humanity, through chambers and courtyards, past walls and obstacles which separate him from his goal. The journey takes thousands of years, the Emperor is long since dead, and yet the message has still not been delivered. For the messenger is still forcing his way through the outer courtyards of the palace. It is not his fault: he is indefatigable. It is simply the "realistic" drawback of physical space-time and mass. The multitudes of people, the myriad obstacles, the vast distance to traverse. And he has still not left the palace grounds.

> ...and if at last he should burst through the outermost gate—but never, never can that happen—the imperial capital would lie before him, the center of the world, crammed to bursting with its own sediment. Nobody could fight his way through here even with a message from a dead man. But you sit at your window when evening falls and dream it to yourself. [49]

And yet is it enough to dream? Kafka is apparently arguing that because of the limitations of time and space, reality in itself can never be known, consequently it can only be dreamed of although it concretely exists. But is this not pressing too far into fantasy? On the level of everyday existence do not sensory perceptions "practically" reveal reality? Where space is not a substantial factor, and thus time delay is infinitesimal, cannot one safely trust one's senses? This would indeed be the case were it not for the fact that the senses themselves are guilty of distortion. In his book, Subliminal, physicist Leonard Mlodinow explains how "Philosophers have for centuries debated the nature of 'reality,' and whether the world we experience is real or an illusion. But modern neuroscience teaches us that, in a way, all our perceptions must be considered illusions. That's because we perceive the world only indirectly, by processing and interpreting the raw data of our senses."[50] Not only must "apparent" reality convey itself through a questionable signal-medium, but once the sensory receptors receive the message they then proceed to systematically warp its form and meaning. The distortion is not slight, but can occur to such a

48. Franz Kafka, The Complete Stories (New York: Schocken Books Inc., 1971), p. 4.
49. Ibid., p. 5.
50. Leonard Mlodinow, Subliminal: How Your Unconscious Mind Rules Your Behavior (New York: Pantheon Books, 2012), p. 45.

degree that one is actually visualizing illusions. The process of lateral inhibition in the limulan eye is a case in point.

Psychologists H.F. Hartline, F. Ratliff, and W.H. Miller discovered an unusual phenomenon in the eye of Limulus (the horseshoe crab). An objective physical process was found to be directly responsible for creating subjective illusions, and hence for misrepresenting reality. The process is that of the lateral inhibition of receptor nerve cells.

A single ommatidium (one eye of the limulan compound eye) is illuminated, creating a series of impulses sent to the optic nerve. The frequency of the impulses is directly related to the intensity of the light. However, as adjacent ommatidia are illuminated the frequency of the original ommatidium consequently decreases. The inhibitory mechanism is formed by an interconnecting "lateral plexus" which maintains contact with each individual eye. Thus one eye's excitation is dependent not only upon its own stimulation, but also upon the stimulation of the surrounding compound eye.

The human eye, while not compound, was found to work upon similar lateral-inhibiting principles. The individual ganglion cells take the place of each component of the limulan eye and operate on sensitivity to their "center" regions and their "surround." Illumination of the center produces excitation of the ganglion cells while illumination of the surround decreases the center's response. The result of the optic structure is the production of non-existent Mach bands which are, in effect, subjectively "real" illusions.

The brightness-contrast effect is created when a pattern of light suddenly shifts from low to high intensity. At the beginning of the field's increasing light, the ganglion cell's surround will receive more illumination and hence inhibit the center's activity. Thus there will "appear" a band of light darker than the intensity really present. On the other hand, at the end of the field's increasing light, the ganglion cell's surround will receive less illumination and hence excite the center's activity. Thus there will "appear" a band of light brighter than the intensity really present.

> ...what you see does not correspond to the physical intensity distribution of the retinal image. The pattern you perceive exaggerates the abrupt transitions in physical intensity across the pattern...
> ...Thus, our perceptions of patterns of light are imposed upon us in part by the center-surround

organization of the retina and in part by the effect of
lateral inhibition operating in these receptive fields. [51]

In effect one is physically geared toward misperceiving reality.
The physical intensity of the actual light can be objectively measured
with a light meter. And yet the human eye will subjectively distort
the perception so that unreal brightness-contrast effects will appear
to exist. Furthermore, the electrochemical activity of the ganglion
cells will also physically parallel the "illusory" subjective perception
of both unseen and nonexistent light. Hence, the processes of
lateral inhibition and center-surround response are tangible physical
correlates for subjective illusions.

Apparently any epistemological theory based upon the perception
of sensa will ultimately fail, for regardless of whether such phenomena
are real, the sensory receptors themselves cannot be trusted. As has
been demonstrated scientifically and maintained by mystics and
ascetics for thousands of years: the senses are not only "filters" of
reality, but also, in fact, actually "liars." Thus both phenomenalism
and representative realism, being based upon the perception of sensa,
are necessarily inadequate and doomed from the start. But are these
the only possible approaches? The shadowy dream of phenomenalism
or the dreamy shadows of representative realism? A more refined
metaphysical theory must consequently be "conceived."

---

51. Philip Groves and Kurt Schlesinger, Introduction to Biological Psychology
(Dubuque, Iowa: Wm. C. Brown Company Publishers, 1979), pp. 242-243.

SECTION TWO

The Transcendental Approach

> *WOMAN:* *Every once in awhile, you wake*
> *up and realize you've spent your*
> *life sleeping.*
> *FIRST MAN:* *I'll only dream when I'm*
> *awake. From now on, that's the*
> *way it'll be. I understand now.*
> *I'll never waste my dreams by*
> *falling asleep. Never again...* [52]

---

52. Eugene Ionesco, <u>Man with Bags</u> (New York: Grove Press, Inc., 1975), p. 134.

Idealism:
Reality as a Concept

---

*"Every man's world picture is and always remains
a construct of his mind and cannot be proved to
have any other existence."* [53]

According to the philosophy of idealism, life may indeed be
analogous to a dream, for all that one knows are the interactions of
the mind—abstractions divorced from tangible substance. Idealism
maintains that all that can be experienced are concepts, and that there
is <u>no</u> existence apart from these concepts. Objective reality as such
does not exist except through one's knowledge or consciousness of
it. The noumenon in itself does not exist. The phenomenon in itself
does not exist. For one is dealing with a realm composed solely of
thought. Schopenhauer advocates this philosophical approach at the
outset of his voluminous work, <u>The World as Will and Idea</u>:

> "The world is my idea:"—this is a truth which
> holds good for everything that lives and knows,
> though man alone can bring it into reflective and
> abstract consciousness. . . .
> It then becomes clear and certain to him that
> what he knows is not a sun and an earth, but only an
> eye that sees a sun, a hand that feels an earth; that the
> world which surrounds him is there only as idea, <u>i.e.</u>,

---

53. Erwin Schrödinger, <u>Mind and Matter</u> (Cambridge: Cambridge University
Press, 1958), p. 44.

only in relation to something else, the consciousness, which is himself. [54]

Idealism thus overcomes the drawbacks of phenomenalism and representative realism by denying the primacy of sensa in determining reality. Its most famous proponent, George Berkeley, believes that the essence or reality of objects lies solely in their being perceived. The tree falling in the forest with no sentient being around to hear, makes no sound, nor without eyes to see does it even fall. Without anyone or anything capable of perceiving, the external world (and therefore the tree) is essentially non-existent. For, according to Berkeley, "Their esse is percipi, nor is it possible they should have any existence out of the minds of thinking things which perceive them." . . ."All things that exist, exist only in the mind, that is, they are purely notional." [55]

Idealism, in its "subjective" as opposed to its "objective" form (the differences will be clarified later), holds that the basis of reality exists solely within the mind. The problem of distortion by both senses and sensa is thus circumvented by regarding only mental impressions as real. However, the question now arises as to which impressions are real and which are false, and how one can differentiate if reality stems solely from the mind. Hence the problem of false data is simply transferred to a problem of false concepts. For if reality is merely "conceived" (as is the premise of "subjective idealism") then which of the myriad subjective realities can one take to be real? Or are all such individual conceptions true? And hallucinations? And madness?

---

54. Arthur Schopenhauer, The World as Will and Idea, vol. 1 (London: Kegan Paul, Trench, Trübner, & Co., Ltd., 1981), p. 3.
55. George Berkeley, "A Treatise Concerning the Principles of Human Knowledge" in Edwin A. Burtt The English Philosophers from Bacon to Mill (New York: Random House, Inc., 1939), pp. 524 & 533 respectively.

Subjective Idealism
Hallucinations and Madness as Real?

"But I don't want to go among mad people,"
Alice remarked.
"Oh, you can't help that," said the Cat: "we're
all mad here. I'm mad. You're mad."
"How do you know I'm mad?" said Alice.
"You must be," said the Cat, "or you wouldn't
have come here." [56]

The problem of subjective idealism stems from its very premise: that reality is a concept without basis in external noumena. Thus all that exists are subjective conceptions which cannot be differentiated by a standard frame of reference. A phenomenological approach may therefore be in order, for there is no way to distinguish reality from hallucinations and madness. All are experientially valid phenomena regardless of whether or not they are objectively real. Indeed, who is to say what is objectively real? The individual or society? Common sense would favor society. But what if reality is consensus insanity? What of the Cheshire Cat's Wonderland where everyone is mad? And what of simple dogmatism? Giordano Bruno was burned at the stake for adhering to the belief in a non-geocentric universe. Galileo was forced to crawl across the church courtyard in repentance for his abominable lies: that the surface of the moon was irregular and not "perfectly" smooth as the heavens should be, that the planet Jupiter had moons, that the sun had spots, that Saturn had rings, and worst of all heresies—that the Milky Way was actually composed of stars,

---

56. Lewis Carroll, <u>Alice's Adventures in Wonderland</u> (New York: Random House, Inc., 1946), p. 73.

myriad stars of which the sun was but one! Galileo was berated as a heretic, liar, cohort of the Devil, and finally reprimanded mildly by his friends as a simple hallucinator. But who was hallucinating?—and what?—and if so, then what is real?

The position of Juhasz and Sarbin, in their article "The Social Psychology of Hallucination,"[57] is that hallucinations are necessarily a social phenomenon. Their reasoning is that it takes at least two or more individuals in order to define an experience as hallucinatory. On the one hand you must have the so-called "hallucinator," the one who is supposedly perceiving something unreal. On the other hand you must have an invalidator, someone who can evaluate and invalidate the perception as unreal. Juhasz and Sarbin's position is that hallucinations must by nature be a social phenomenon—one person experiencing, one person invalidating. And the problem now becomes apparent: who is to judge what is objectively real?—for any number of invalidators will still compose a subjective framework.

One person may see a ghost. Others may claim that it is simply imagination. However the question arises: what if, in the final analysis, ghosts are actually real? In that case the so-called hallucinator was in fact perceiving reality, whereas the invalidators, the ostensibly rational and clear-minded individuals were, in effect, misperceiving or misinterpreting or simply being blind to the "real" truth.

In primitive societies an entire tribe may serve as the standard of reference. But in their case such tribes may contrarily reinforce the perception of ghosts. The problem is: who is to determine which basis of reference is true? Is the individual's experience of the supernatural to be labeled "imaginary" and "hallucinatory" here in western civilization, only to be relabeled "true" or "visionary" in South America or Tibet?

The point is obvious. In the long run does it make any difference what is imagined and what is real? Might not the two be the same? Could it be possible that the mystics are right?—that life is a dream, and all we take as real only an illusion? Dream and reality would then be only semantic classifications totally arbitrary and meaningless and ultimately without sense. Could what psychiatrist John Lilly proclaims be true?

> "In the province of the mind what one believes to be
> true either is true or becomes true within limits to be

---

57. Theodore R. Sarbin & Joseph B. Juhasz, "The Social Psychology of Hallucinations" in "Journal of Mental Imagery," 1978, 2, pp. 117-144.

found experientially." Later I was to realize that the limits of one's beliefs set the limits of the experiences. At the limits of one's creative imagination (whatever that is!), there are a set of beliefs yet to be transcended. The learning process is on a vast scale. [58]

In the province of the mind, there are no limits. [59]

Hence, although hallucinations cannot be objectively verified they nevertheless remain subjectively valid, that is in so far as the mind itself—ones own internal experience—is also experientially valid though objectively unverified, physically non-existent, and thus only conceptually or "heuristically" or idealistically real. Regardless of definition, the experience of dreams, hallucinations, or even waking consciousness is valid only in terms of the subjective meaning it conveys. Therefore fantasy and imagination are equally as meaningful as "real" life. For whether an experience is totally subjective or objectively real is of no consequence since such a determination can never be confirmed.

In his short story "The Other" the South American writer Jorge Luis Borges proposes that life may be a dream, but that one must simply accept it since it is all that one has, all that one knows. The plot is of a return to the past and a meeting with "The Other"—one's youthful past self. In an attempt to understand their paradoxical dilemma, both "selves" consider the possibility that they are dreaming each other's presence. One self may be dreaming of a nonexistent future. On the other hand, one self may be dreaming of a nonexistent past. The metaphysical problem can never be resolved, and so each self must simply resign himself to an acceptance and affirmation of the dream.

> "Perhaps we have stopped dreaming, perhaps not. Our obvious duty, meanwhile, is to accept the dream just as we accept the world and being born and seeing and breathing."
>
> "And if the dream should go on?" he said anxiously.
>
> To calm him and to calm myself, I feigned an air of assurance that I certainly did not feel. "My dream

---

58. John C. Lilly, The Center of the Cyclone (New York: The Julian Press, Inc., 1972), pp. 17-18.
59. Ibid., p. 5.

has lasted seventy years now," I said. "After all, there isn't a person alive who, on waking, does not find himself with himself." [60]

Hence all that is important is that the experience is considered real. The subsequent understanding and insight, whether correct or mistaken, will consequently have a profound impact on one's life, one's own "subjectively" real life. It may be a fallacy to base one's world-outlook upon a possible illusion, but when life itself may be an illusion what more can be done?

And yet the drawback of subjective idealism is that as the world appears, so it is. By changing one's mind or conceptions the universe in turn follows suit. Thus the hallucinations of psychotics are justifiably real, for anything one conceives is subjectively valid. There is no standard framework except the general consensus of society, and such consensus is often not only proven to be wrong, but also varies cross-culturally and contradicts. Hence there is no certainty even with mankind as a whole. There is no certainty even within one's own mind. For objectivity is an illusion, and subjectivity is too. And so one comes to a metaphysical abyss within a world of tentative reality, which is in effect tantamount to a world of unreality. Incipit the dream . . . (of life?) . . . Here begins the fall . . .

In the strange story "Tlön, Uqbar, Orbis Tertius" Borges explores the metaphysical ramifications of subjective idealism through a literally "conceptual" work of fiction. The plot is of the greatest undertaking ever carried out by man—the conception of a new world. The vast enterprise is accomplished by means of the insidious warping of knowledge. A multimillionaire funds a secret group of scholars, scientists, engineers, and artists in a project whose goal is to create an imaginary world. The principles composing the conceptual framework must be valid and consistent in forming a cohesive whole. They must be strict and coherent and yet allow for the widest scope of expression. The fundamental basis of reality chosen?—subjective idealism.

Beginning with the plan's prototype, accounts of an imaginary land are subtly bound together within otherwise-exact reproductions of The Encyclopedia Britannica. The adulterated copies are then planted in used-book shops throughout the world. And yet the dissemination of imagination in the guise of truth is not enough. In

---

60. Jorge Luis Borges, The Book of Sand (New York: E.P. Dutton, 1977), pp. 13-14.

the plan's second phase an entire volume of an "alien" encyclopedia makes its appearance. The massive work recounts the legends, the history, the science, the philosophies, the arts, and the culture of an alien society.

Borges then becomes masterful in his manipulation of the paradox. Within the "conceptual" framework of the imaginary world, the ingeniously self-reflecting encyclopedia begins discoursing on the problems of subjective reality and epistemology! The effect is literally mind-boggling, for the foundation of this imaginary world is the premise of subjective idealism—that reality is a concept without basis in external noumena. Hence there is no "thing-in-itself," but only states of perception which fluctuate with thought. What one conceives as real is therefore real, and consequently the imaginary encyclopedia along with its imaginary civilization is a self-justification of its own existence, its own autonomous reality. Hence, spontaneous creation.

An uncanny episode is subsequently related. Experiments are conducted to determine the creative power of the idealistic mode of thought. Prisoners are offered freedom if they unearth the tombs of an ancient civilization—a fraudulent civilization which they are fooled into believing. As would be expected the first digs fail to uncover the remains. But on a subsequent dig the supervisor unexpectedly dies. Ancient objects are immediately unearthed along with a corpse and a tomb. Hence it is realized that "knowledgeable" witnesses can impede the "idealization" of objects. A reality based upon subjective idealism is thus ambiguous and yet dynamic in its tentative projections.

> Things become duplicated in Tlön; they also tend to become effaced and lose their details when they are forgotten. A classic example is the doorway which survived so long as it was visited by a beggar and disappeared at his death. At times some birds, a horse, have saved the ruins of an amphitheater. [61]

The alien culture begins to invade the earth. Enamored by a world order, a cosmos infinitely more logical and sophisticated and meaningful than its own, mankind slowly adopts the Weltanschauung of Tlön. Reality is transformed into an imaginary vision. Apparently the concept of existence based upon subjective idealism just happens

---

61. Jorge Luis Borges, <u>Labyrinths</u> (New York: New Directions Publishing Corporation, 1964), p. 14.

to coincide with the universal order. Material objects from the alien planet consequently appear and merge with the "projection" of earth. The language and customs of Tlön gradually find their way into the minds of men and supplant those of humanity.

> The contact and the habit of Tlön have disintegrated this world. ...Already the schools have been invaded by the (conjectural) "primitive language" of Tlön; already the teaching of its harmonious history (filled with moving episodes) has wiped out the one which governed in my childhood; already a fictitious past occupies in our memories the place of another...A scattered dynasty of solitary men has changed the face of the world...
> ...The world will be Tlön. [62]

Thus the relative framework of subjective idealism results in a whimsical reality dominated by consensus opinion or even consensus insanity. Perhaps the Cheshire Cat is correct in assuming that "we're all mad here." Perhaps nothing more can be done but to hallucinate and to dream. Hence a world of subjective reality is equivalent to a world of unreality. Without a tangible basis of reference, an objective reality or noumena, existence disintegrates into nothing more than a dream, a common dream at best, but a tenuous dream all the same.

Therefore subjective idealism, while capable of conceiving, is incapable of sustaining. It is inadequate in dreaming a new reality for life, for in its subjective manifestations it will become dissipated and more than likely lead to madness. A more "objective" approach is consequently needed in order to recreate the world.

---

62. Ibid., p. 18.

Objective Idealism
Life as a Real Dream

---

*"The dream reveals the reality, which conception
lags behind."* [63]

— *Franz Kafka*

When thoughts dictate reality life becomes equivalent to a dream.
When the mind knows no boundaries imagination runs amuck,
abandoning consciousness to the realm of madness. Thus without
a standard frame of reference the mind cannot form a basis from
which to interact. The individual, if strong enough, can experience a
meaningful subjective reality, but more than likely the "total" freedom
will degenerate consciousness through lack of discipline and stable
order.

Objective idealism differs from subjective idealism in that, while
both accept the premise of the primacy of mind in conceiving reality,
objective idealism acknowledges external noumena which manifest
the concepts, whereas subjective idealism denies the "thing-in-
itself," maintaining that it is all a product or composition of thought.
Objective idealism is hence realist as regards epistemology while
subjective idealism is anti-realist. And yet both are idealist as regards
metaphysics. The drawback of subjective idealism is thus rectified by
objective idealism's affirmation of external reality. One therefore has
recourse to a standard framework in conceptualizing or interpreting
the universe anew.

The fallacy of psychotics, ascetics, and "ivory-tower idealists" is
that they minimize the validity of objective reality. Withdrawing into
one's subjective reality and/or madness may be justified if there is no

---

63. Janouch, op. cit., pp. 55-56.

external basis, for then one can function however one chooses. But the problem with madmen is that they must be taken care of; they are dependent upon the material world; they surrender their fates to the control of others. Hence they are imprisoned, tortured, murdered, and sometimes, God forbid, even cured!—cured by being drugged into acquiescent stupor, having portions of their brains removed, or collectively fried through electroshock therapy.

The same interdependence is true of mystics and ascetics. It is one thing to deny Maya (the illusion of life) and entomb oneself in a cave in order to confront the "real" spiritual world. It is another to leave a small gap in the wall through which food and water can be passed—"necessities" handled by a dedicated servant standing vigil for months or (in cases of extreme "renunciation") even years.

Finally it is one thing to conceive bold new plans, dream amazing new ideas, envision a utopian world of the future—and another to act upon those concepts amidst the harsh reality of life. The classic "ivory-tower idealist," the Hindu ascetic, and the Belleview nut, may very well be content within their own private subjective realities, but if the bombs ever drop they too will find themselves burning up in the same "objectively real" puff of smoke.

Thus the problem with subjective idealism is that it is totally subjective, which is inconsistent with the external world of facts. Hence in a country spiritually idealist (e.g. India) millions have died of famine, disease, and the general afflictions of poverty. Whereas in countries basically realist (e.g. the United States) wealth, health, and affluence are the general rule. Consequently an alternative approach must be assumed in order to bridge the two seemingly contradictory worldviews. Both are justifiable in and of themselves, but both are inadequate and negated without the other. Hence a stopgap must be conceived in order to fuse the dichotomy into a complementary whole. Such a stopgap is the sophisticated approach of objective idealism—an approach which combines the subjective idealist's view that life is a dream with the realist's view that life is tangible and real, forming one paradoxically cohesive view that life is essentially a "real" dream.

What is astonishing is that, whereas other metaphysical and epistemological theories are simply debatable speculations, the objective idealist philosophy is proving true in many areas of science. Research in quantum physics, psychology, stereoscopy, astrophysics, and physiology all have reality indices within objective idealism. Hence this temporary "stopgap" may very well be the fundamental principle of existence.

If objective idealism is indeed the structural basis of the universe, then external reality exists and manifests itself to the perceiver who subjectively conceptualizes the information within an idealized framework. Or in other words, the mind does not simply perceive, but rather idealizes the world so as to make it conform to its own expectations, its own framework of reality. Hence there is an active participation, a metaphysical interaction between the subjective observer and the objective world. The so-called perceiver actually projects his conceptions into his vision of the world then passively interprets his own subjective version of reality—a version which does not necessarily correspond to the objective impressions he receives, nor with the versions of other subjective observers. This ability of the mind to structure and validate its own reality has been demonstrated scientifically. Experimental research on binocular perception is a case in point.

Psychologists John Ross and John Hogben of the University of Western Australia discovered an unusual factor involved in binocular depth perception. Stereoscopic vision, which is characteristic of most higher forms of life, apparently employs an anticipatory conceptual framework which results in an idealization of reality. Building upon the work of Bela Julesz, Ross and Hogben used computers, oscilloscopes, and random-number generators in order to analyze the components of binocular vision. Subjects viewed the images of two separate oscilloscopes, one oscilloscopic pattern for each separate eye. A random-number generator selected coordinates for flashing points of light and their counter-points on each screen. The results were amazing.

What appeared monocularly as a random flashing of lights became, when stereoscopically combined and manipulated, vivid geometric figures "apparently" suspended three-dimensionally in space. The figures themselves do not really exist. They are two-dimensional monocular images projected ideally into the subjective visual process. All that exists in reality are two separate sets and series of random light flashes in motion. The stereoscopic image produced is not objectively real, but simply subjective idealizations or literally "constructs of the mind." "To see a scene produced by random-dot stereograms for the first time is an uncanny experience. Objects stand free in space, vivid and sharp-edged." [64]

One method of creating such binocular illusions is to set a region

---

64. John Ross, "Scientific American," March 1976, Volume 234, Number 3 (New York: Scientific American, Inc., 1976), p. 82.

of the random-dot screen into motion. With the aid of a computer, a selected portion (e.g. a square) of the visual field is shifted in one direction while the oscilloscopic image of its counterpart is shifted opposite. Both displays viewed monocularly show only flashes of light moving against a dark background. But viewed stereoscopically the images are "subject" to the grand metamorphosis of three-dimensional illusion. Ross explains the effect:

> At the center of the display a square appears to float in front of the background. The square is like a sheet of dark plastic on which points of light move about. Although the pattern of points of light on the surface changes continuously, the square itself presents a solid and unchanging appearance. Binocular perception has constructed the solid square (which is actually not there) in order to account for the information it is receiving from the random-dot stereograms. [65]

However, what is most interesting is not the creation of subjectively idealized illusions, for these are an unnatural artifice of experimental manipulation of the senses. Rather, what is important is the information obtained by experimenting with these projections. Analysis of the components of binocular perception reveals astonishing insights into the mental construction of reality. Apparently there exists within the visual system something akin to an independent mind or mental faculty capable of making complex decisions. The subliminal process somehow scans visual input; extracts information on depth, motion, and aesthetic qualities; determines which of (at least) two separate modes of vision will be utilized; adopts that mode; then finally projects the resultant image into the mind—all before the perceiver is conscious of what he sees!

Several uncanny aspects of stereoscopic vision were discovered. Through experimentation in the binocular combination of photographs of two different faces, previous investigators detected a decided improvement in beauty. "The selective blending that occurs in binocular combination indicates that the visual system apparently has the ability to accept or to reject information on aesthetic grounds."[66] While this may itself not alarm one's sensibility, it will when one considers that this process is occurring spontaneously and

---

65. Ibid., p. 82.
66. Ibid., p. 80.

automatically, naturally with one image and not merely artificially with two, continually every instant one looks binocularly at the world. It is one thing to consciously choose to see life "ideally"; it is another to be geared or forced unconsciously to do so.

Another interesting aspect of binocular vision is that the idealized images distort the perception of external reality. The points of light composing the three-dimensional square are trapped within the edges of the "subjectively" raised plane. They cannot move across the idealized definition of depth which actually does not even exist. Monocularly viewed, both oscilloscopic images show patterns of light-points moving about uniformly without interference from subjectively imposed barriers. But when the idealized constructs of binocular perception are imposed this free-flowing movement of light-points is not the case.

> Instead they seem to bounce back from the edges of the floating square. What this means is that the visual system attaches functional significance to the edges constructed by the binocular process, and that motion across such edges from one depth level to another is prohibited. Furthermore, when monocular perception conflicts with binocular constructs, the monocular percepts are suppressed. [67]

Another interesting factor in binocular perception is the ability to geometrize spatial configurations. When the computer designates two surfaces within the same region one might expect an indistinguishable overlap or merging and blurring to appear. But with the sophisticated idealization of stereoscopic vision this is not the case.

> ...the result might be expected to be chaos, but it is not...The problem of making both surfaces visible is elegantly solved by the visual system: the surface in front appears to be transparent and the one behind opaque. This shows that there is an intuitive grasp of spatial relations built into binocular perception that transcends mere geometry. [68]

67. Ibid., pp. 82-83.
68. Ibid., p. 83.

Perhaps the strangest aspect of binocular vision is that it has two separate modes of depth perception it can employ. In an experiment investigating lateral tracking, counter-point images were delayed in appearing to one eye. This procedure mimics the eyes' time delay of background and foreground images while following a moving object. Delays below 50 milliseconds resulted in a static depth scene caused by the normal spatial disparity process. However delays above 70 milliseconds resulted in an uncanny streaming or spiraling effect. The target object (theoretically in motion) is suspended motionless three-dimensionally in space while foreground lights stream in one direction and the background lights stream opposite. The effect parallels the phase differences of images appearing in the two optic fields' pursuit of laterally moving objects. A shift from static to streaming occurred when the time interval was between 50 and 70 milliseconds.

Thus it is obvious that binocular perception has recourse to two totally separate modes of vision while tracking objects in motion: spatial disparity and phase difference. Furthermore it can also tap two totally separate sources of information. Delays in static images for more than 50 milliseconds results in a collapse of depth impression, for the mind cannot collate disparity information at longer intervals. Despite the fact that the light-point image lasts for 130 milliseconds it still, although visible, cannot be contrasted with its counter-point. However with delays in streaming an equally paradoxical contrast occurs, but with exactly opposite effects. At delays above 70 milliseconds phase differences can be detected which results in the impression of depth. This is acceptable since it is simply a switch from one perceptual mode to another, all taking place while the contrasting counter-points are still visible. However, at 130 milliseconds and as high as 2,000 milliseconds the counter-points which carry disparity information are no longer visible. Thus the visual system now has recourse to records which need no present contrast in order to perceive depth. Hence in the case of static depth scenes, information cannot be extracted even while contrasting points are still visible. While, on the other hand, in the case of streaming depth scenes, information is extracted from images no longer present to be contrasted (obviously contrasting with an intricate memory system unavailable to the static depth process).

I believe we must conclude that binocular perception has access to records of visual input that are independent of what we see. This represents a radical break with the commonsense view that what we see constitutes all the sense data from which higher perceptual processes develop a conception of the scene before our eyes. It appears there are records of visual input that can be consulted before anything at all is seen in order to determine the proper framework for perception. [69]

Thus research in the most important of the five senses reveals that vision may be based upon objective idealist principles. Reality exists in the form of objectively real light-images which manifest themselves to the subjective perceiver. However the perceiver actively idealizes reality by consciously or unconsciously fitting information into conceptual frameworks of reference. Hence, experiments in advanced stereoscopy seem to vindicate the premise of objective idealism. John Ross thus concludes the article with the metaphysical implications of his work.

What we observe in random-dot stereograms may well be idealized conceptions, imposed on the external flow of information by something within the visual system. What we observe may be a structure built by vision when it adjusts itself as it tunes in to the sources of the information it can sense. Just as a computer has a program, so may the visual system have a program of arrangements for shapes in space and time. What we see is an interpretation of the external world, ordered within a framework the visual system imposes because of the attitude it adopts. In other words, we adopt a perceptual attitude in order to comprehend the world. [70]

One's view of reality is thus heavily influenced by one's subjective perception. The mind is preset to idealize the world—even to the point of creating illusions for enhancement. Reality is ignored, glossed over, made prettier and more intelligible. Some may argue that these results are an artifice of unnatural conditions. After all, random-dot stereograms do not occur in nature. One's vision was simply tricked by feeding different images to each eye. But the human visual system is replete with further examples under natural conditions. One such

69. Ibid., p. 85.
70. Ibid., p. 86.

example is the illusion of peripheral color vision.

Color can be perceived only by light receptors known as "cones" which are concentrated in the fovea of the retina. Receptors known as "rods" surround the fovea for peripheral vision, but these rods can perceive only shades of black and white. In reality it is physically impossible to perceive color outside the central field. But the mind reinterprets and smoothes over the disparity.

> The illusion of full colour outside the central image is provided by the brain. This can be demonstrated by moving a previously unseen object into a person's field of view. The person is unable to identify the colour until the object is close to their main image area. [71]

Objectively we should see color only directly in front in the area of focus. Vision to the sides should appear as black and white. But instead we see (or think we see) color everywhere. It is a delusion that we insist on taking for reality. Our mind creates the illusion of peripheral color simply because it is aesthetically more appealing.

A related delusory phenomenon is created by the blind spot. Rods and cones (visual receptors) do not exist at the point where the optic nerve attaches to the retina. A small blind spot should appear in the visual field of both eyes. Instead, the mind extrapolates visual data from surrounding receptors and smoothes over our picture of the world.

This blind spot can be easily demonstrated in the optical illusion experiment of the "suspended hotdog." Hold both hands at arms-length with forefingers pointing at each other a few inches apart. Focus both eyes at the point in between. Slowly bring both fingers toward each other. Suddenly the tips of both fingers appear to magically join with space on either side. It looks like a "suspended hotdog" because the blind spots in both visual fields cut off the finger-tips from both hands as well as from both arms. According to Professor Susan Greenfield:

> Our visual perception is based only partly on external reality—the brain makes up the rest as it goes along... The brain is not merely a passive recipient of nerve

---

71. John Downer, <u>Supersense</u> (London: BBC Books, 1988), p. 52.

signal patterns sent from the eyes. It learns to make endless assumptions, short cuts, and extrapolations, so the apparently seamless scenes we see are partly guesswork. [72]

Leonard Mlodinow agrees and further emphasizes that these processes are of an involuntary or "subliminal" nature:

> The world we perceive is an artificially constructed environment whose character and properties are as much a result of unconscious mental processing as they are a product of real data. Nature helps us overcome gaps in information by supplying a brain that smoothes over the imperfections, at an unconscious level, before we are even aware of any perception. [73]

> That's what our unconscious processing does for us— it creates a model of the world. [74]

A further example of natural distortion in the human visual system occurs with "perspective." Aesthetically pleasing illusions are created by the mind in order to retain a stable perspective of the world. We conceptually distort objective reality to fit our mold of what should be seen. In his book, <u>Inventing Reality</u>, physicist Bruce Gregory describes a practical demonstration of this phenomenon.

> Stand at the foot of a tall building, point a camera upward, and take a picture. The picture will look badly distorted—it could hardly be called accurate. Yet there is nothing wrong with the camera, and cameras normally do not lie. We have a convention about how photographs of buildings "ought" to look, and this photograph violates that convention. The apparent distortion in the photograph tells something about what we "really" see. The visual world is not a

---

72. Susan A. Greenfield (general editor), <u>The Human Mind Explained</u> (New York: Henry Holt and Company, Inc., 1996), p. 94.
73. Mlodinow, <u>op. cit.</u>, p.50.
74. Mlodinow, <u>op. cit.</u>, p. 45.

faithful reflection of the images on the retinas of our eyes but a world somehow constructed out of such images.

...How much of what we see is similarly an "optical illusion"—an interpretation fabricated from our interaction with the world? [75]

Neuroscientist V.S. Ramachandran agrees with this view in his book, The Tell-Tale Brain.

Indeed, the line between perceiving and hallucinating is not as crisp as we like to think. In a sense, when we look at the world, we are hallucinating all the time. One could almost regard perception as the act of choosing the one hallucination that best fits the incoming data, which is often fragmentary and fleeting. Both hallucinations and real perceptions emerge from the same set of processes. [76]

---

75. Bruce Gregory, Inventing Reality (New York: John Wiley & Sons, Inc., 1990), pp. 1-2.
76. V.S. Ramachandran, The Tell-Tale Brain (New York: W.W. Norton & Company, Inc., 2011), p. 229.

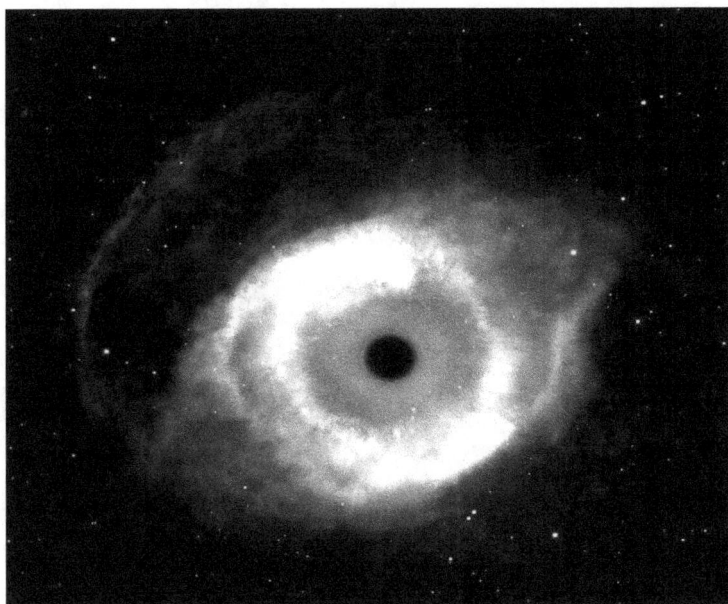

Helix Nebula in the constellation Aquarius—700 light years away.

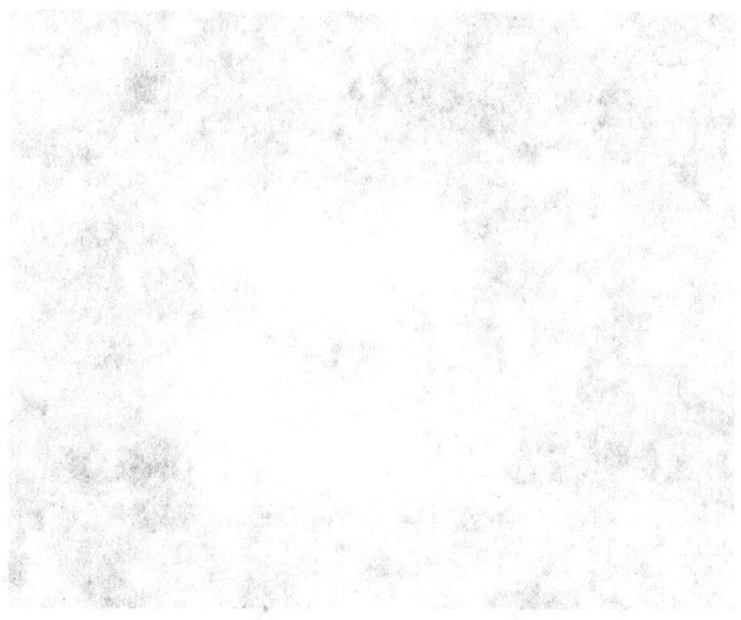

Objective Idealism and Advanced Physics
An Interaction Between Subjective & Objective Reality

"The Mind is it's own place, and in itself
Can make a heav'n of hell, a hell of heaven..." [77]

— *Satan*

The metaphysical ramifications are immense. Modern science is verging on a reconception of the world. Advances in physics, cosmology, psychology, and physiology tend to support the premise of an interconnecting causality of perception between the observer and the observed. In other words, the observer is not a mere passive recipient of sensory stimuli. Nor, on the other hand, is the universe an "objectively" static generator of such stimulation. Rather, there appears to be an interaction between the subjective perception and the objective manifestation. The universe as such is relative and in flux.

Physicists are well aware of the ambiguous nature of energy and matter—the two basic components of physical reality. It seems impossible to separate the subjective from the objective perception, for what one senses is in part determined by the way in which one senses. The observer, in effect, interacts with, alters, and perhaps even creates what he perceives. According to Heisenberg's "Uncertainty Principle" knowledge of an object's nature can only be attained through methods which necessarily alter that object's nature. According to the wave-particle duality of light, energy behaves sometimes as a wave and sometimes as a particle depending solely upon the situation and one's

---

77. John Milton, <u>Paradise Lost and Paradise Regained</u> (New York: Airmont Publishing Company, Inc., 1968), p. 17.

point of view. According to Einstein's "Theory of Relativity" there is no absolute perceptual nature of reality, but only relative frames of references from which to view the universe.

Reality is thus influenced by the subjective state of the observer and not totally dependent upon the external universe itself. It is not simply a matter of an absolute universal state being viewed through myriad subjective standpoints, for as Einstein has clearly demonstrated, there is no absolute state. Rather, it is a case of innumerable relative frameworks overlapping and interacting, constituting the universe as a whole. Hence reality is, at least in part, actually determined by the conditional nature of the observer. Categories of subjective and objective thus no longer apply. And Niels Bohr, pioneer of quantum theory, wholeheartedly agrees:

> The impossibility of distinguishing in our customary way between physical phenomena and their observation places us, indeed, in a position quite similar to that which is so familiar in psychology where we are continually reminded of the difficulty of distinguishing between subject and object. [78]

The meaning is clear. Relativity and quantum mechanics have revolutionized man's conception of space-time reality. The universe is consequently not what it appears, for each individual and each perceptual entity lives or exists within its own subjective reality, its own subjective frame of reference. Reality is thus relative, and each individual is trapped within his own isolated conception, his own "dream" of life. And yet the possibility nevertheless exists for an interaction of "dreams."

Einstein's Special Theory of Relativity is based upon the principle that nothing can travel faster than the speed of light. Light is thus a limiting factor which, in effect, produces time. Without light as a limitation, time would not exist. Consider this, for example: a causal event (e.g. a supernova gamma-ray burster) occurs in one part of the galaxy, producing an effect (destruction of all planetary life) after a period of a hundred years, a hundred light years away in space. If the speed of light were not the "speed-limit" of the universe then the following could occur. At twice the speed of light an effect could be

---

78. Niels Bohr, Atomic Theory and the Description of Nature, Volume 1: The Philosophical Writings of Niels Bohr (Woodbridge, Connecticut: Ox Bow Press, 1987), p. 15.

transferred fifty years ahead of the destructive light (high intensity electromagnetic radiation or gamma rays), arrive on the planet and forewarn the populace fifty years before the time of their impending doom. At ten times the speed of light the same effect could be produced ninety years ahead of time. At one hundred times the speed of light—ninety-nine years ahead of time. And so on ad infinitum with the cause and its effect drawing closer together until finally, with an infinite speed, the cause and its effect will be simultaneous. The situation would be impossible according to the principles of even modern advanced physics. And yet faster-than-light travel has been observed to occur—the object, signal, or medium of transmission being as yet unknown. The phenomenon is known as the Einstein-Podolsky-Rosen effect and has been experimentally recorded in numerous laboratories throughout the world. What it questions is the very nature of physical reality.

The phenomenon is briefly described as follows. A pair of protons is generated simultaneously. The polarization on one is spin-up. The other proton has a complementary polarization of spin-down (this is the only way two protons can coexist, it being impossible for both to be spin-up or spin-down.) The protons are then forced apart in opposite directions. One proton is caught in a screen spin-detector and its spin is determined to be up or down. At the same moment the other proton, perhaps halfway across the galaxy, has also had its spin determined. For if the spin of the trapped proton is up, then the other proton's spin must necessarily be down. And if, on the other hand, the trapped proton's spin is down, then the spin of its counterpart must necessarily be up. Thus knowledge of an existing state in an entirely different part of the universe can be determined by measuring a totally separate and physically isolated condition (a violation of quantum mechanical premises itself). Information has thus traveled not only faster than light, but at an infinite speed, having been transferred simultaneously without the intervention of space. And this is impossible according to relativistic physics, for not only physical matter, but any communication, knowledge, or signal is restricted from surpassing the speed of light.

What is in violation is apparently the principle of "Einstein separability" which is at the heart of man's commonsense view of the world. According to "Einstein separability" or "Einstein locality" no influence (whether physical interaction or non-physical communication) can travel at speeds faster than light. Hence physical laws necessarily forbid influences over distances which require superluminal interactions. But this is apparently just what is taking place! And the paradox has not yet even theoretically been resolved.

Einstein, Rosen, and Podolsky attempted to demonstrate, in their hypothetical experiment, the inadequacy of the quantum-mechanical approach. But what they actually succeeded in demonstrating was not only the inadequacy of quantum theory, but also that of relativity. The paradoxes abound. According to quantum mechanics it is impossible to have knowledge of an existing state without in some way interacting with and consequently disturbing that state. The observation must necessarily interfere with the condition being observed. Hence absolute measurements of a phenomenon are objectively impossible. For example, the measurement of an object's position renders its velocity proportionally indeterminate (and vice versa). The measurement of a phenomenon's energy similarly renders its time span proportionally indeterminate (and vice versa). These limitations of knowledge are not a result of inadequate observational techniques, but rather an inherent or "metaphysical" limitation of observation itself. Thus the very interaction of the observer with the observed consequently renders all measurements either inadequate or invalid.

Einstein and his colleagues were dissatisfied with this "uncertain" or "indeterminate" nature of reality. They argued that the universe was deterministic, but only appeared indeterminate because of certain "hidden variables" that were presently unknown. Thus they developed the Einstein-Podolsky-Rosen effect in an attempt to discredit one of the major premises of quantum mechanics: that the observer and the observed are inextricably intertwined. What this experimental effect demonstrates is that knowledge of an existing state can be logically determined by the use of inductive reasoning alone, without the necessity for physical observation. In the double-proton experiment, the spin of the second proton was fully determined without the necessity for observational interaction. While still in flight both protons were indeterminate in their spins, but once the first proton had been detected and determined, so too had the second. Follow-up detection served only to confirm the already known spin. This experimental finding is hence contrary to one of the basic premises of quantum theory.

Niehls Bohr, a proponent of quantum theory, maintained that the Einstein-Podolsky-Rosen effect was not inconsistent with quantum mechanics, but was simply a fallacy of logic on the part of Einstein and his colleagues. Bohr explained that the flaw in the E-P-R effect lay in the interpretation of determinacy. According to quantum mechanical logic the spin of the second proton is actually still indeterminate until the moment of its actual detection and subsequent determination. Hence the so-called "knowledge" of the isolated system was merely a probable tendency and not a certainty. Thus Bohr avoids the commonsense view of the situation by retreating to an abstract premise of logical positivism which states that speculations on unobserved conditions are totally meaningless. But is it meaningless? When the predictability of a condition reaches one hundred percent probability common sense would relegate the outcome to a certainty. Who is being unrealistic? Einstein or Bohr?

But Einstein himself ran up against an equally humiliating paradox which threatened to undermine his special theory of relativity. The relativists could not subscribe to the indeterminacy of quantum theory. They could not align themselves with a view which held the universe to be tentative and in flux based upon a foundation of random occurrences. According to Einstein the spin of the second proton cannot be "indeterminate" but is simply unknown. At all times and all places, regardless of detection, both proton's spins must be fully determined. The "hidden variables" are all that hold man from such knowledge. Thus reality exists independent of human conception and in a fully deterministic state. Such is the inductive reasoning implicit in Einstein's realism. But such a commonsense approach became itself open to doubt. The theoretical gadfly was known as "Bell's theorem or inequality."

Bell proved mathematically that, even if "hidden variables" did exist, the deterministic theory of the relativists could not be sustained unless they allowed for influence at a distance between either particles or detectors.

> That communication would sometimes have to be accomplished at a speed faster than the speed of light, and hence it would violate not only the locality condition but also the special theory of relativity.[79]

And yet this is exactly what is being observed. Follow-up experiments have confirmed the quantum-mechanical interpretation. The general consensus among physicists is that quantum expectations have been fulfilled. The subatomic universe does appear to be operating along the lines of quantum theory, thus violating Einstein separability and perhaps the special theory of relativity as well. There

---

79. The editors (?), "Esse Est Percipi" in "Science and the Citizen," <u>Scientific American</u>, July 1978, Volume 239, Number 1, p. 78.

is however an alternative explanation.

One manner of avoiding a violation of Einstein separability is to redefine the concept of superluminal signals. The principle of forbidding faster-than-light communication is an integral part of the special theory of relativity. Without it the entire framework of relativity would collapse, for the speed of light is a universal constant which plays a fundamental role in man's conception of reality (e.g. E=MC squared). One possible recourse is to restrict the superluminal speeds to "meaningful" communication or signals. Thus the faster-than-light influence between the two protons can be considered the result of an automatic effect between two interacting phenomena which have a common cause. There need be no transfer of "meaningful" information. But as Bernard d'Espagnat explains in an article in Scientific American:

> Even this solution impairs scientific realism to some extent. The basic law that signals cannot travel faster than light is demoted from a property of external reality to a feature of mere communicable human experience. [80]

Hence scientific realism itself ultimately falls back upon a framework of subjective conceptions rather than objective reality. And as such it loses its power of conviction. The entire realm of modern physics consequently remains paradoxical and unresolved.

If quantum mechanics is correct then the universe is indeterminate and possibly an indivisible whole. But what about the realistic determinism manifested in the Einstein-Podolsky-Rosen effect? On the other hand, if Einstein's realistic determinism is correct then the universe is composed of myriad subjective and relative frameworks which, nevertheless, are totally determinable. And yet what about Bell's theorem which either violates Einstein separability or makes it extremely untenable? The contradictions and weaknesses exists within both quantum and relativity theories. And yet there is no resolution in sight. According to Gary Zukav in his book, The Dancing Wu Li Masters:

> Bell's theorem not only suggests that the world is quite different than it seems, it demands it. There

---

80. Bernard d'Espagnat, "The Quantum Theory and Reality" in Scientific American, November 1979, Volume 241, Number 5, p. 180.

is no question about it. Something very exciting is happening. Physicists have "proved", rationally, that our rational ideas about the world in which we live are profoundly deficient. [81]

Or as physicist Evan Harris Walker explains in <u>The Physics of Consciousness</u>:

Stitch by stitch, the whole fabric of reality, so carefully woven together by classical physicists, was unraveled into a plethora of confusing facts. Matter was not matter but waves and energy, the stuff of no more than motion. Waves of light were as much particulate as waves of energy. And neither space nor time had any more than a relative meaning. There ceased to be any cohesive picture of reality. Physics had run out of pictures to explain its tapestry of colors. [82]

81. Gary Zukav, <u>The Dancing Wu Li Masters</u> (New York: William Morrow and Company, Inc., 1979), p. 309.
82. Evan Harris Walker, <u>The Physics of Consciousness: The Quantum Mind and the Meaning of Life</u> (Cambridge, Massachusetts: Perseus Publishing, 2000), p. 49.

Universal Fiction:
An Attempt at a Resolution of Thought & Reality
using Light as a Catalyst

"Now, my suspicion is that the universe is not only queerer than we suppose, but queerer than we can suppose." [83]

Modern physics is in a quandary. Either the universe is tentative, nonobjective, and indeterminate or else instantaneous actions at a distance can occur. If the quantum-mechanical interpretation is correct then the spin of the second proton, though one hundred percent probable, can only be said to be determined when actually detected. If Bell's theorem is correct then faster-than-light influences can occur which will violate causality, Einstein locality, and the special theory of relativity itself. In either case, something is drastically wrong with man's conception of the universe. Or as Bernard d'Espagnat concludes in his article on "The Quantum Theory and Reality":

> The violation of separability seems to imply that in some sense all these objects constitute an indivisible whole. Perhaps in such a world the concept of an independent existing reality can retain some meaning, but it will be an altered meaning and one remote from everyday experience. [84]

Nobel laureate, Niels Bohr, explains that the quandary both relativity and quantum theory face may be the same: the idealization

---

83. J.B.S. Haldane, <u>Possible Worlds and Other Papers</u> (New York: Harper & Brothers Publishers, 1928), p. 298.
84. <u>Op. cit.</u>, d'Espagnat, p. 181.

of perception compounded by the speed of light and the uncertainty of the quantum world.

> In spite of many points in which they differ, there is a profound inner similarity between the problems met with in the theory of relativity and those which are encountered in the quantum theory. In both cases we are concerned with the recognition of physical laws which lie outside the domain of our ordinary experience and which present difficulties to our accustomed forms of perception. We learn that these forms of perception are idealizations, the suitability of which for reducing our ordinary sense impressions to order depends upon the practically infinite velocity of light and upon the smallness of the quantum of action. [85]

The resolution of the paradox may lie within the nature of light. Light, or electromagnetic energy, is itself a paradox. It behaves sometimes as a wave and sometimes as a particle, depending upon one's point of view. It defines the speed limit of the universe, and thus preserves the notion of causality. No physical body can travel at the speed of light. And yet light, in its particle aspect (the photon) has energy and consequently mass (E=MC squared), but only while in motion.

The paradox is that light has an indeterminate mass (hence it can be bent by gravity as has been experimentally proven), and yet it can move through space without expending energy, for light is energy. And yet, according to Einstein's special theory of relativity, any physical body approaching the speed of light will also tend to become infinitely massive. But light does not. It remains virtually unchanged unless acted upon from without. Something is obviously wrong in our understanding of light and the answer may lie within its subjectively interpretable nature.

According to Einstein's special theory of relativity, physical objects are not only restricted to subluminal (slower than the speed of light) velocities, but their combined speeds when moving away from or approaching each other are also restricted to subluminal velocities. In other words, whereas subatomic particles can travel at ninety percent the speed of light, two subatomic particles can never travel away from

---

85. Bohr, op. cit., p. 5.

each other both at ninety percent the speed of light, for otherwise they would be separating at 180 percent the speed of light in clear violation of relativity physics. Hence the combined "separation" or "approach" velocities of physical objects can never equal or surpass that of light. But why is this so? Why should the nature of two different systems be altered simply because of their perspectival relationship to each other?—a relationship which does not necessarily involve physical interaction. It is a paradox which cannot be conventionally explained.*

Furthermore, the conventional summation of velocities does not

---

* *This is a baffling and paradoxical situation. According to Einstein, separation velocities between objects can never combine to equal or surpass the speed of light. The reason is that all frameworks or reference points are relative. There is no objective framework from which to judge or measure. For this reason, no one can say which object is standing still and which is moving away. All one knows and can measure is the motion between the two frameworks. And this motion can never equal or surpass the speed of light for physical objects.*

This is a principle of relativity. This is Einstein. However this seems absurd. Linear accelerators send particles to speeds approaching that of light. Can't one accelerator shoot particles in one direction, while another accelerator next to it sends particles in the opposite direction? Would not those particles be separating at a combined velocity greater than light? This thought experiment is actually feasible (albeit costly). Two adjoining linear accelerators end-to-end. According to relativistic principles the particles in both accelerators should never exceed 50% the speed of light. What would the particles do, slow down close to half the speed of light because they know the other particles are also separating at close to 50% the speed of light? And if they did slow down, wouldn't that violate Einstein Separability? How could knowledge of two different systems influence each other at speeds infinitely close to the speed of light? And if Einstein Separability isn't violated, then the two opposing accelerators would be propelling particles away from each other faster than the speed of light which is also a violation of relativity.

Another baffling situation: hold two lasers end-to-end. the beams are emitting light in opposite directions. Aren't the beams separating at twice the speed of light? And doesn't light have a mass component in the form of photons (E=MC squared)? And even forgetting the restriction of objects separating faster than light. Even in their energy form, relativity still says the ultimate speed limit in the universe is that of light. This is counter-intuitive. Does that mean the light from both lasers have slowed to half the speed of light so that they don't separate faster than the speed of light? But they are light, and they can only travel at the speed of light—in both directions.

Relativistic jets are observed in supermassive black holes and active galactic nuclei. Each jet is emitting particles at close to the speed of light in opposite directions. Aren't those particles separating faster than light?

Quasar 3C 273 itself is showing a superluminal motion of 9.6 the velocity of light inside its inner jet. Many physicists believe this an optical illusion due to an observational effect from viewing the jet slightly off-angle. However other physicists disagree. Some believe superluminal motion does occur and that the evidence is mounting because the off-angle line of sight explanation is not great enough to skew the measurements to such a degree.

Guth's Inflation Theory (which many astrophysicists support) holds that in the early universe faster than light velocities were possible.

In a complementary finding, Perlmutter, Schmidt, and Riess believe the accelerating expansion of the universe may exceed that of light in the farthest reaches of the universe (which is closest to the Big Bang).

Some cosmologists are now allowing for space itself to expand faster than the speed of light, but only restrict objects from being propelled greater than the speed of light. This, they believe, will save relativity from being violated.

However, could this not be a semantic juggling of terms? In deep space galaxies have been measured separating at from four to six times the speed of light. Some scientists believe this to be an illusion due to angular, observational effects. Others believe this may be due to the accelerating expansion of the universe in deep space. By the time the light reaches us, space has expanded the apparent distance between the galaxies. They didn't really separate that fast, they only look like they did.

This bizarre paradox is unsettling. Something is missing from our understanding of relativity, the conditions of deep space, and of the early universe.

apply to light. For example, a radiating object traveling at 90 percent the speed of light does not radiate its light in front at 190 percent the speed of light, and radiate its light in back at 10 percent the speed of light. Such addition and subtraction of velocities simply do not apply to the paradoxical nature of light. For light (and any form of electromagnetic energy) must always travel at the speed of light, no more, no less. This paradox can be resolved by realizing that light is neither a wave nor a particle, but rather a force or medium capable of infinite mutability.*

According to commonsense Newtonian physics, light should gain momentum while radiating from an object moving forward in space, and lose momentum in the opposing direction. But this does not take place. Instead what happens is that light gains energy (not momentum) as it radiates from an object moving toward an observer, and loses energy as it radiates from an object moving away from an observer. The change is therefore not in speed but intensity. The phenomenon is known as the "Doppler Effect" and more commonly as the "red shift" when applied to electromagnetic radiation from receding objects in space. The problem is that this phenomenon is entirely subjective or relative in both its perception and manifestation. For example, it makes no difference whether it is the observer or the light source which is moving away from or toward the other. All that matters is the original light intensity and the relative motion between the two frames of references. Or as William Kaufmann explains in The Cosmic Frontiers of General Relativity:

> The exact amount by which the wavelength of a source is shifted directly depends on the relative speed between the source and the observer. If the speed is low, the shifting will be only slight. If the speed is very high, the shifting can be enormous. For example, imagine approaching an ordinary light bulb at 99.99 percent the speed of light. At such a high speed, the shift toward shorter wavelengths is so great that the light bulb seems to be emitting X-rays. Similarly if you were to move away from an ordinary light bulb at 99.99 percent the speed of light, you could detect only radio waves from the light bulb. In either case, although the light bulb really gives

---

* *The following theory and thought-experiment is adapted from Part Two: Looking-Glass World in the essay "Through the Cosmic Looking-Glass: The Relativistic Nature of Energy and Light" in Alcheringa: A Metaphysical Alchemy by Wayne Omura.*

off only visible light, you could not see the light bulb with your eyes. [86]

Thus light, or electromagnetic energy, is actually a warped phenomenon. It has no absolute reality, but only myriad apparent or relative realities viewed from myriad subjective frames of reference.

Light can theoretically move forever (within a vacuum) without altering its nature or expending energy. However in reality light is continually losing and gaining energy depending upon the framework of observation.

Consider the following hypothetical situation. Two rocketships are traveling along the same axis of motion at 99.99 percent the speed of light. The man in the leading rocket (A) is looking backward at the rocketship (B) following behind which has a searchlight attached to the bow of the ship. As long as both A and B are maintaining the same speed (99.99 percent that of light) they will remain within the same relative frame of reference. Consequently A will see normal visible light emanating from the searchlight of B.

But then suddenly something happens. "A" develops engine trouble and his rocketship quickly begins slowing down. However A is unaware as he watches calmly out of the rear of his ship. Suddenly A realizes that something has gone wrong, for the searchlight of B has become increasingly intense. First growing in brightness it then disappears from vision and A's instruments show that he is being bombarded by "black light" (or ultraviolet radiation). As A slows to a halt, B's searchlight is now bombarding him with high intensity X rays. And yet the searchlight as B sees it is only radiating normal light. Under continual exposure to X rays A will soon suffer radiation sickness unless he repairs his engine and accelerates to the same relative framework as that of B.

"A" eventually repairs his engine and accelerates back to 99.99 percent the speed of light, but in the opposite direction! He has accidentally set his engine in reverse and is now heading directly for B. And yet he has no need to worry about collision, for his ship will be destroyed long before impact. It will be destroyed by the radiation emanating from B's conventional searchlight. The increasing frequency or intensity of B's searchlight will have traveled through ultraviolet through X rays to gamma rays—the most powerful electromagnetic radiation in the universe. While combined light

---

86. William J. Kaufmann, III, <u>The Cosmic Frontiers of General Relativity</u> (Boston, Toronto: Little, Brown and Company, Inc., 1977), pp. 39-40.

velocities between approaching physical objects is strictly forbidden by relativity, it still allows for a close approximation. Thus the two rocketships traveling toward each other both at 99.99 percent the speed of light will approach at a combined speed very close to, but not exceeding, that of light. The result is that the extremely compressed or intensified radiation from B's searchlight (in the form of gamma radiation) will set up an antimatter field somewhere between A and B which will react with A's rocketship and A himself in a catastrophic antimatter explosion. "A" and his rocketship will be annihilated. William Kaufmann explains the creation of antimatter from gamma radiation:

> Nuclear physicists can create matter and antimatter most easily from high-energy gamma rays.... under appropriate conditions a gamma ray can spontaneously turn into a particle and an antiparticle. This process occurs only if the gamma ray possesses a great deal of energy, more energy than is contained in the matter of the particles it creates. [87]

As is well-known from science-fiction stories and confirmed by scientific fact, antimatter and matter will react in a violent catastrophic explosion when brought together. Hence A's rocketship as well as A himself will be annihilated by the searchlight of B—a searchlight "really" projecting only harmless visible light. The effect of Doppler-shifting is thus totally subjective, and yet it is real! For A is now disintegrated simply as a result of his relative frame of reference. In other words A no longer exists simply because of his subjective perception or condition. His point of view has, so to speak, resulted in his destruction.

And yet, although B's searchlight has played the role of a deadly ray-gun, it has not changed in and of itself. While A is being disintegrated by the searchlight, B can stick his hand directly in front of the light and nothing will happen. For B is still within the same frame of reference as his "gun." What is to A a dangerous weapon is to B simply a searchlight which reflects ordinary light from the surface of his hand.

The problem is where is this antimatter field "really" located? Certainly not projecting from B's searchlight, for otherwise B could not stick his hand in front without being "burned." Certainly not in the

---

87. Ibid., p. 245.

intervening space between A and B, for another rocketship traveling at 99.99 percent the speed of light between A and B (following B's line of motion while slightly ahead) will again see only harmless light radiating from B's ship. The antimatter field must hence reside solely at the subjective framework of A, and not anywhere in between. It is a reality shared only by those within the same relative perspective.

Light or electromagnetic energy is hence a subjectively manifested and perceived phenomenon with no absolute nature of its own. It is paradoxical, almost an illusion, and yet it is real—real because of its tangible effects upon the objective world, an illusion because it "appears" differently and is different to different observers. And yet light or electromagnetic energy is the sole information carrier in the universe. All that we know is ultimately derived either directly or indirectly from electromagnetic radiation. Even sound waves or gravitational effects are synaptically transformed into electrochemical impulses to the brain. Thus man is trapped within an inherently paradoxical framework from which he cannot escape—a framework so indeterminate and whimsical that it is akin to a dream . . .

Wave-Particle Duality:
The Infamous Double-Slit

"Anyone who is not shocked by quantum theory has not understood it." [88]

— *Niels Bohr*

Perhaps the most impressive physical evidence for this indeterminate, holistic universe is Thomas Young's well-known "double-slit" experiment. No tangible, repeatable experiment illustrates the paradoxical nature of light so convincingly. What it proves to classical physicists is the irrefutability of the wave-particle duality of electromagnetic energy. What it suggests or proves to quantum physicists is a holistic interconnection in the universe. In either case the phenomenon is baffling.

The experiment is surprisingly simple, but the results are complex and as yet not fully understood. A light-source projects light onto a screen. An intermediate screen is placed between the light and the original screen with a vertical slit through which the light must pass. The result is a band of light appearing on the original screen which is consistent (more or less) with a "scatter-pattern" for light's particle or photon nature.

Now open a second slit parallel to the original slit. Light shining through the double-slit shows an interference pattern on the original screen. Waves of light spreading out from each slit are mixing together and interfering. This is confirmation of light's wave nature and a denial of its particle nature. So far there is no inconsistency.

The problem arises with subsequent openings and closings of the

---

88. Niels Bohr, <u>The Philosophical Writings of Niels Bohr</u>, (1998) as quoted through Karen Michelle Barad, <u>Meeting the Universe Halfway</u> (Durham, North Carolina: Duke University Press, 2007), p. 254.

double-slit. Close the left slit and leave the right slit open. The result is a scatter-pattern showing no wave nature, no interference. Now open the left and close the right. The result is once again a scatter-pattern showing no wave nature. Now open both slits. Surprise! Light shows an interference pattern resulting from its wave nature. The pattern of light on the original screen is different than from that of both left and right scatter-patterns combined. In other words, photons or energy quanta are striking the back screen in a far different manner when both slits are open than when either slit is closed and the results are combined.

To classical physicists there was nothing unusual about this phenomenon. Light was merely interacting and interfering as it passed through both slits. But a major problem developed with the advent of quantum mechanics, particle physics, and modern technology. For it became apparent that it was not simply a case of light interacting, but an actual switch from scatter-patterns to interference patterns: an instantaneous switch from particle to wave nature. Conventional physicists maintained that this simply proved the baffling dual nature of light. This was merely the classic case for wave-particle duality. But to quantum physicists this was no longer explanation enough.

For one thing, the intensity of light can be decreased to such an extent that only one quantum of energy is projected at the screen at a time. In essence, photons or electrons (remember this substitution is allowed because of Einstein's principle of mass-energy equivalence) can be fired one at a time as particles. With both slits open a barrage of photons or electrons will show the interference pattern. (This makes some sense since at least there are other particles present with which to collide.) But an interference pattern also shows up by firing photons or electrons one at a time over a long period of time. And here is one problem: with what is the solitary particle colliding to create the interference?

A photon or electron can pass through only one slit. Restricted to its particle form, light is physically confined in space to passage through one (and only one) opening. In fact, detectors can actually count each passage and impact of electrons as a "click." And a photographic plate can record the exact impact of each photon. And here is the second problem: how does an individual photon or electron "know" whether or not the slit is open?

Slowing down the rate of firing to one quantum at a time allows for no interaction between particles passing through either slit. No interference pattern should result because only one particle was present in the experimental apparatus at any give time.

Common sense dictates that only a simple scatter-pattern should be seen behind each slit. But this is not the case! If both slits are open an interference pattern occurs. If either slit is closed there is a scatter-pattern behind the remaining open slit.

How does this happen? As a particle is fired it can pass through only one slit. There are no other particles present to interfere with its path. The particle moves through one open slit and is flying toward the back screen. Nothing should interfere with its projectile path. But something does. Whether or not the second slit was open determines where the particle will land. If the second slit was open the particle will "adjust" its flight path and "act" as though it has interfered with other "possible" "imaginary" particles.

In more graphic terms, with only one slit open a band of light will appear on the screen directly behind either slit. Nothing will appear between the two slits unless both slits are open. If both slits are open, the single solitary particle will be deflected from its normal particle trajectory and land somewhere between the two slits. In effect, though projected as a particle, it will manifest results consistent with that of a wave. On the other hand, if the second slit was closed, the particle will remain true to its original course and strike the back screen in a scatter-pattern consistent with its particle nature.

The mind-boggling question is: how does the electron or photon or energy quantum or particle "know" whether or not the second slit is open? Somehow it does, for it adjusts its flight path accordingly. The condition of the second slit can be changed at the last instant, but the particle cannot be fooled. Whether or not the second slit was open at the very instant of passage through the first slit determines where the particle will impact. Logic and conventional physics cannot explain this phenomenon—"a phenomenon which is impossible, <u>absolutely</u> impossible, to explain in any classical way,"[89] according to Nobel Prize-winning physicist Richard P. Feynman. In fact, even more astonishing results can be obtained by refining the experimental apparatus. According to astrophysicist John Gribbin:

> We can try peeking, to "see" which hole the electron goes through. When the equivalent of this experiment is carried out, the result is even more bizarre. Imagine an arrangement that records which

89. Richard Feynman, Robert Leighton, and Matthew Sands, <u>The Feynman Lectures on Physics, Volume III</u> (Reading, Massachusetts: Addison-Wesley, 1981), p. 1.

hole an electron goes through but lets it pass on its way to the detector screen. Now the electrons behave like normal, self-respecting everyday particles. We always see an electron at one hole or the other, never both at once. And now the pattern that builds up on the detector screen is exactly equivalent to the pattern for bullets, with no trace of interference. The electrons not only know whether or not both holes are open, they know whether or not we are watching them, and they adjust their behavior accordingly. There is no clearer example of the interaction of the observer with the experiment. When we try to look at the spread-out electron wave, it collapses into a definite particle, but when we are not looking it keeps its options open. [90]

In other words, keeping both slits open, but with recording devices at each slit, destroys the wave-interference pattern. The mere monitoring of an electron as it passes through either slit confines it to its particle nature. Scatter-patterns will develop behind each slit even though both slits are open! And this is simply because the experimental apparatus has "defined" and recorded the energy source as a particle rather than as a wave. The ambiguous wave/particle has been pinned down and can no longer fool us. It must now revert to a particle and behave accordingly.

Physicist John Wheeler maintains that these results support his concept of a "participatory universe." Reality is defined by a meshing of subject and object. The observer plays a requisite role in the nature of the reality discovered. The experimenter finds astonishing results because he himself set up astonishing conditions. There really shouldn't be that much room for surprise, for man is an active agent in what he perceives.

In any case, what is incredible about the double-slit experiment is that Einstein separability seems to be clearly violated, for knowledge of separate states is being passed instantaneously. The particle seems to know instantly the condition of the other slit (a speed faster than light which is a contradiction of the theory of relativity). No conventional explanation for this phenomenon is convincing. Instead, a rash of bizarre proposals abound. For example: the particle splits

---

90. John Gribbin, In Search of Schrödinger's Cat (New York: Bantam Books, Inc., 1984), p. 171.

in two, passes through both slits, and recombines upon impact. Or, the particle is really only a probability wave which can pass through both slits at the same time and interfere with itself. Or, the particle is real, but is guided by a "ghost wave" (Einstein's own speculation). Or that the particle passes back and forth in time and back and forth through the slits until decisions are made and impacts are detected.[91] Or, the wave-interference pattern is an illusion—the result of probability impacts and distribution that take on the appearance of wave-interference. (This last proposal has some merit since a thousand experimental apparatuses in a thousand locations around the world will show an interference pattern distribution when a single particle is fired and the resulting impact distributions are combined. In other words, the recorded impact of just one particle from each of a thousand laboratories around the world will show the interference pattern when plotted together.)

Another bizarre explanation is Paul Dirac's theory that all electrons are really just one electron. Or how about the proposal that subatomic particles have consciousness? Or that they are linked by an acausal connecting principle (Jung's "synchronicity"). Or how about Hugh Everett's "many-worlds" interpretation in which the interference pattern is the interface between alternate realities? The probability waves reflect all possibilities which to Everett are actual multiple realities. The dilemma of how a single particle can interfere with itself is solved elegantly by Everett: the particle is interacting with alternate versions of the event in which the particle actually went through the other slit in a parallel universe. Far from being mere science-fiction fodder, Everett's "many-worlds" interpretation is being seriously considered. Physicist Fred Alan Wolf believes, "although this proposal leads to a bizarre world view, it may be the most satisfying answer yet devised."[92] And Princeton physicist John Wheeler compares Everett's breakthrough on par with Newton, Maxwell, and Einstein: "...nothing quite comparable can be cited from the rest of physics except the principle in general relativity that all regular coordinate systems are equally justified."[93]

In fact John Wheeler himself has added immeasurably to the paradoxes, complications, and confusion. Wheeler elaborated on the

---

91. Victor J. Stenger, <u>The Unconscious Quantum</u> (Amherst, New York: Prometheus Books, 1995), p. 150 & 158.

92. Fred Alan Wolf, <u>Parallel Universes</u> (New York: Simon & Schuster, Inc., 1988), p. 39.

93. John Wheeler, "Review of Modern Physics" Volume 29, p. 464.

double-slit by devising the "delayed-choice" experiment. In brief, the light passes through one or both slits and <u>then</u> the experimenter can change the apparatus so as to "determine" "after the fact" which mode was chosen by the light: particle or wave, one slit or two. In other words, after the light has already passed the slits the experimenter can reach back in time and choose which path it took—after the path has already been taken! This is accomplished through a set of mirrors which delays the recording of the impacts. When the light has already passed through, the experimenter can change the apparatus from one slit open to both open or vice versa. The impact pattern will then follow in accordance with his delayed choice. And yet his choice was made after the light had already passed through the slit or slits! (Incredible as it may seem, a 1985 experiment by Alley, Jakubowicz, and Wickes at the University of Maryland has verified Wheeler's "delayed-choice.") Is the past being determined by the present? Is causality being undermined? According to Nobel laureate Richard P. Feynman, if the ramifications of the "double-slit" experiment could be understood it would clear up half of the problems of quantum physics: "In reality, it contains the <u>only</u> mystery . . . the basic peculiarities of all quantum mechanics." [94]

The History Channel's informative series, "The Universe," delves into the baffling paradoxes of the double-slit experiment. The narrator concludes:

> But one thing is clear. The rules that govern this subatomic world hint at a universe that's just as mysterious as science fiction. In fact, quantum physics may suggest that reality is simply a figment of our imagination. [95]

And Science series "Through the Wormhole" adds further:

> This suggests that we can change the way reality behaves just by looking at it. Does this mean that reality itself is not real? [96]

94. Feynman, <u>op. cit.</u>, p.1.
95. Daniel Snyder (writer and producer), "The Microscopic Universe" from "The Universe: Season Six" (Flight 33 Productions, LLC for History Television Network Productions, 2011 A & E Television Networks, LLC).
96. "How Does the Universe Work?" from "Through the Wormhole With Morgan Freeman: Season Two" (Revelations Entertainment and The Incubator for Science, 2011 Discovery Communications, LLC).

Robert Nadeau and Menas Kafatos propose a new epistemology due to quantum mechanics and conclude:

> Although physical theory has served to coordinate our experience with nature beautifully, we can no longer regard the truths revealed by these theories as having an independent existence. These truths, like other truths, exist in our world-constructing minds. [97]

In any case, no proposed theory seems totally "realistic" or convincing. For rationality is out the window. New-Age physicists point to Young's classic double-slit experiment as strong evidence for a quantum interconnectedness to the universe. Somehow the particle "knows" the conditions of an entirely separate locality. And somehow it is also aware of whether or not it is being observed. If an audience is at hand the particle suddenly takes on a new role. The universe has become a magic theater shifting shapes at whim. It is a holistic, holographically projected universe that is almost a dream.

"Can nature possibly be as absurd as it seems to us in these atomic experiments?" [98]
                                        — *Werner Heisenberg*

---

97. Robert Nadeau and Menas Kafatos, The Non-Local Universe: The New Physics and Matters of the Mind (New York: Oxford University Press, Inc., 1999), p. 190.
98. Werner Heisenberg as quoted by Richard Wolfson in The Great Courses: Einstein's Relativity and the Quantum Revolution: Part 2, Tape 2, Lecture 18: "Wave or Particle?" (The Teaching Company, Limited Partnership, Chantilly, Virginia, 2000).

Holographic Illusions:
The Universe as a "Real" Dream

_____

In One Hundred Years of Solitude Gabriel Garcia Marquez succeeds in creating a work of "real" fiction. Fiction in the sense that the events and characters are figments of the imagination written down by an author. Real in the sense that this written-down fiction is analogous to the physical universe at large. Hence the reality of One Hundred Years of Solitude lies not only in its fictional realness, but also in its real fictitiousness.

Marquez ingeniously incorporates advanced physics and cosmology into the framework of his fiction. A modern alchemist himself, he examines and correlates the implications of science in an attempt to grasp the fundamental basis of the real universe. And he does in fact succeed. With lucid fictional analogies Marquez builds upon the philosophical ramifications of recent scientific breakthroughs and metaphysically relates them to the meaning and purpose of life. The reality of the universe is hence exemplified through fiction. And yet what better mode of narration for a universe that was created? Out of nothingness springs existence? Could imagination not then reign?

The novel is the history of a family from its conception to its end. It is a metaphysical metaphor of the universe from its creation to its doom. Marquez has succeeded in creating a self-contained whole, a microcosm, an entire universe in itself. The fictional narrative is a self-reflective, self-enclosed reality which creates and destroys itself with each beginning and ending. It is real in the sense that it is a living creation, a process that works itself out through its enactment. There is no escape from this paradoxical web of internal fiction entwined within its own fiction which cannibalizes itself as the story progresses. One must simply read on into the labyrinthine structure, hopefully resolving the dilemma before the dilemma resolves oneself. Thus the story is, in its own perverted way, its own creation, its own destruction.

The characters in the novel (the entire family tree) can be envisioned as particles of light moving through the darkness of space. They are trapped within their own solitude, for it is only they themselves who can illuminate the universe. And even then such a universe is only a reflection of their own self. And yet they are searching for their self. They are searching for the light.

The analogy of light as the characters of fiction is the key to synthesizing the novel. Light emanating from a source consists of a dual particle-wave nature. The Buendian characters (the family name) as photon particles are thus individual entities with their own private lives. And yet at the same time they are Buendian archetypes or a wave of the same identical substance. Though photons can be warped by speed and gravity their essential properties remain relatively unchanged. Hence the Buendia clan may appear to vary slightly from individual to individual, but collectively they are simply distorted images of a single essence.

The essence is that of the family novel written by Melquiades, the gypsy, one hundred years ahead of time. Melquiades is the focus of his own creative work of fiction. He is an alchemist who has discovered the key to eternal life, the key to creating his own "real" dream.

The philosophers' stone which Melquiades has discovered is the understanding that light is the only reality. Electromagnetic radiation is the sole carrier of information and it alone is indestructible and eternal. Light may travel billions of light years across the universe and yet remain essentially intact. Thus Melquiades realizes that to become pure energy or quintessential light is, in effect, to become transcendent and immortal. He consequently dies and becomes a ghost, an image or reflection without tangible substance, a hologram of energy without the hindrance of matter. Melquiades has found "The Tree of Life," the "elixir," the "philosophers' stone" and has thereby become immortal.

But what is most interesting is how Marquez weaves fiction and advanced physics into Melquiades' literal "enlightenment," for the elixir which makes Melquiades immortal actually transforms him into light. The transmutation is caused by the realization that the universe itself is made up solely of light. Hence all is illusion, and yet all is equally real. Thus the cinematic reference whereby "the cinema was a machine of illusions" [99] just as is reality and the novel where "living

---

99. Gabriel Garcia Marquez, One Hundred Years of Solitude (New York: Harper & Row, Publishers, Inc., 1970), p. 211.

images"[100] abound, where "the character who had died and was buried in one film...would reappear alive and transformed into an Arab in the next one."[101] This is indeed what Melquiades discovers—that life and reality are analogous to a cinematic film of living light-images which can be played and rerun forever unchanged, for light is an ethereal substance which cannot die.

Life, especially if created, preordained, and authored by God, is analogous to a book written down "one hundred years ahead of time."[102] All is recorded and exists simultaneously within the pages. Hence time does not exist, or rather it exists in one instant of frozen eternity. "Melquiades had not put events in the order of man's conventional time, but had concentrated a century of daily episodes in such a way that they coexisted in one instant."[103]

It is like a universal hologram with all events and images occurring simultaneously superimposed upon one another. The madness emerges when the characters of the novel realize that they are only characters of fiction living out an illusion. They are trapped in time and bounded by gravity. They are prerecorded images immersed within a field of light, and they cannot escape the positive curvature of the universe, a curvature which will make them return to the source.*

Marquez has illustrated the paradoxical nature of modern physics, creating a fictional story about the "real" fictional universe. Reality is a dream structured by thought or imagination, a story or film projected within the theater of the mind. We are alone in our own One Hundred Years of Solitude, for time does not exist, or rather it exists in one simultaneous and eternal instant. Melquiades, and those discovering the philosophers' stone, can escape the eternal projection by becoming a projector themselves, a creator or dreamer of one's own real dream. The novel's history will end, and yet the dreamer will go on...but only if he succeeds in dreaming beyond the boundaries of space-time.

---

* *I know, I know, space is flat. There is no positive or negative curvature to the universe. But this critique was written in 1980 when the shape of the universe was unknown. It's still a great metaphor so I am leaving it in case the universe decides to start curving.*

100. Ibid., p. 211.
101. Ibid., p. 211.
102. Ibid., p. 382.
103. Ibid., p. 382.

Rene Magritte. *The Human Condition.* 1933

Metaphysical Holography

Although itself a "mere" work of fiction, <u>One Hundred Years of Solitude</u> is nevertheless a clear analog of life, both in its objective and subjective manifestations. In the objective realm the physical components of the universe, energy and matter, can be viewed as eternal "projections," wave forms in constant flux, a cosmic hologram in perpetual motion. On a less physical, more intangible level—that of the mind—consciousness and perception can be regarded as a holographic interpretation, an interference pattern which becomes, and is itself, thought. In the subjective realm dreaming can be seen as an integrating function of consciousness, the projection of a more holistic self. Thus the best description of both subjective and objective reality is in the form of a holographic dream, waves of consciousness and energy interacting to create the pattern known as life. (The following is an explanation of dreaming developed by the author.)

The Metaphysical Hologram of Dreams
Part One: The Isolation Factor

There is an isolation factor to dreaming. As the individual descends into stage 4 deep sleep he loses awareness of the external world as well as awareness of inner mental activity. It is as though he is being steadily drained of volition and consciousness, as though he is being "deadened" and withdrawn from external reality. Indeed, experimental studies show that the sleeper has become increasingly difficult to awaken whether through sounds, lights, or stimulating electrodes to the brain. But eventually the individual emerges from the depth of sleep, as though ready to reawaken, to reenter the world. His consciousness and body reactivate for the ascent, but they awaken not to reality, but rather to a dream. And he engages in this dream "as though" it were real. What is important is that REM-dreaming is always preceded by a cyclical descent into deep sleep,* and that this cycle is repeated four or five times throughout the night. It is as though the individual's mind is being metaphysically brainwashed, as though one's consciousness or self is being opened or "made clean."

With an ever-growing time-span since initial sleep onset, the dreamer finds himself increasingly dissociated from reality. With a continual series of "awakenings" into strange dreams, he finds it harder and harder to discriminate reality, to discriminate himself. He begins simply to accept whatever his rambling subconscious has to offer. And what he accepts becomes ever-more fantastic. According to psychologist Ann Faraday in her popular book, <u>Dream Power</u>, evidence indicates that "dreams tend to become more dramatic

---

* *The sleep disorder known as "narcolepsy" is an exception to this rule. Narcoleptics characteristically fall directly into a REM period without having to first descend and ascend the stages of sleep.*

and bizarre and to contain more childhood material as the night progresses."[104] Dr. Frank Freemon corroborates this on a physiological level by noting that later REM periods have greater eye movements, greater variations in pulse and blood pressure, and are associated with more vivid dreaming. Freemon concludes that later REMs are apparently more associated with psychological changes rather than mere physical renewal.[105]

Furthermore, later REM periods are typically longer than earlier REMs, and are so psychophysiologically intense that hospital personnel consider the predawn hours the "fatal" ones. For it is during this time that patients undergo severe stress and anxiety, resulting in physical complications and distress (many heart attacks take place during this period of sleep.) There is an obvious momentum to REM dreaming, a build-up very likely due to an increasing dissociation from the external world. Thus the isolation factor serves not only as a circuit breaker to the flow of external reality, but also as a hypnotic catalyst in transforming imagination into the "real." But for what purpose? Of what value is such radical dissociation of the psyche? What meaning is there in believing imagination to be real?

---

104. Ann Faraday, Dream Power (New York: Berkley Publishing Corporation, 1972), p. 83.
105. Freemon, op. cit., p. 158.

The Metaphysical Hologram of Dreams
Part Two: Dreams as a Hologram of Consciousness

As one passes through life, one passes through many "selves," many phases and stages of psychosocial development. These past selves are as much a part of one's total psyche as one's current self, but the ego tends to deny and repress their existence. Infant, child, adolescent, and man, and all the transformative selves in between. They are all one being. But the current ego, in its egotism, prefers to consider itself as all, as a totally independent and self-created identity. It disowns its past. It disowns its true being.

But during sleep the ego consciousness gradually loses its hold. One loses touch with the external world and thus one's ego lacks confirmation. Affirmative feedback is missing and so one's ego diminishes. The self or the ego literally dies in deep sleep. But it is resurrected as one awakens in the dream. The only difference is that now it is a conglomeration of the self, an interaction or hologram. It is not limited or confined to one's current state, but can roam freely through the multiplicity of its being. It is no longer hampered by egotistical conceptions. It can explore all possible avenues of thought. The infinite perspectives of life are within its scope. It is like a kaleidoscope of life, an intricate collage of perspectives, ever-shifting, ever-changing in meaning and hue. And what's more, this collage is not confined to an infinitely perspectival past, but can move freely into the possible future, can explore the full range of impossible imagination. One can experience the dream as though a child, as though an old person, as though an animal, or a deranged murderer. Any viewpoint is possible within the dream.

Thus dreaming serves as an integrative function of consciousness. It is a hologram of perspectives combined in one mind. What is experienced during the day, one's thoughts, feelings, and worries are played upon and reinterpreted within a more holistic mind. Consciousness grows richer. One's self becomes more.

Perception as a Holographic Interface:
An Interference Pattern within the Mind

_____

One's perception of reality can itself be considered an interference pattern of energy—a holographic construction within the mind. All forms of perception are, either directly or indirectly, the result of wave phenomena impinging upon the brain. Vision results from visible electromagnetic radiation reflected from external objects onto the retina of the eye. The sense of heat results from invisible infrared radiation detected by sensory neurons in the skin. Hearing results from compressed air waves vibrating against the basilar membrane in the inner ear. Touch, taste, and smell result from neuronal discharges traveling as electrical impulses in a wave front to the brain.

As mentioned earlier, sensory stimulation is tantamount to an illusion. The experimental evidence of lateral inhibition in the limulan eye as well as the human brightness-darkness contrast in the phenomenon of Mach bands indicates that the visual process cannot be trusted. The study on binocular depth perception further demonstrates that what is "seen" by the eye is not necessarily an accurate reflection of what is objectively present. Indeed, the entire spectrum of electromagnetic energy (the sole information carrier in the universe) is subject to distortion. The phenomenon of Doppler-shifting mentioned previously shows that all electromagnetic waves are perspectival in nature relative to the observer. And this Doppler-shifting applies equally to sound waves affecting hearing. Audition is thus also the victim of perspectival distortion.

Furthermore, studies on tactile sensation also show the same susceptibility to wave frequency distortion. An experiment conducted by G. von Békésy in 1967 indicates that even touch is basically a frequency analyzer. Békésy used a pair of vibrators to stimulate the tips of two fingers. Stimulation took the form of two series of rapid clicks. When the clicks in either finger were delayed for more than three or four milliseconds the subject, as would be expected, felt separate clicks in both fingers. However, when the clicks were delayed for about one millisecond, only one series of clicks was felt in the finger that received the stimulation the earliest. When the time between clicks was reduced lower than one millisecond an even stranger phenomenon occurred. The clicking moved into the open space between the two fingers! Sensation was "felt" in an area where no sensory receptors existed! Békésy concludes that "This matter of the external projection of vibratory sensations seems to be strange and hard to believe, yet it is well known in many fields."[106] Thus even in the more tangible realm of tactile sensation, wave frequency distortion results in subjective illusions. Hence even what one feels is not necessarily real.

This phenomenon of wave distortion and holographic illusions penetrates into the very mechanics of the mind. The neurophysiology of the brain is based upon an interconnecting network of neuronal synapses which propagate electrical impulses as a form of communication. Electrical activity within the brain occurs as actual rhythmical waves which can be detected and studied by the electroencephalograph. These brain waves are generated in different areas of the brain in varying frequencies dependent upon one's state of consciousness. But in general it is a more diffused and "holistic" process. Brain waves from various sensory receptors merge to comprise a single wave function—a wavefront synthesizing diverse elements into a whole. "In fact, information from any sense organ must potentially be capable of integration with that from any other."[107]

John Eccles, in his article on "The Physiology of Imagination," considers the brain "as one great unit of integrated activity"[108]—ten billion neurons each of which receives input from a hundred other neurons and sends information to a hundred more.

> Thus we have envisaged the working of the brain as a
> patterned activity formed by the curving and looping
> of wavefronts through a multitude of neurons, now

---

106. G. von Békésy, Sensory Inhibition (Princeton: Princeton University Press, 1967), pp. 220-26.
107. John Eccles, "The Physiology of Imagination," Scientific American, September 1958, volume 199, number 3, p. 141.
108. Ibid., p. 136.

sprouting, now coalescing with other wavefronts, now reverberating through the same path—all with a speed deriving from the millisecond relay time of the individual neuron, the whole wavefront advancing through perhaps one million neurons in a second. In the words of Sir Charles Sherrington, the brain appears as an "enchanted loom where millions of flashing shuttles (the nerve impulses) weave a dissolving pattern, always a meaningful pattern, though never an abiding one; a shifting harmony of sub-patterns." [109]

Although such an integrative description of brain physiology is reminiscent of holographic theory, Eccles himself refutes such a theory on technical grounds. The brunt of this new paradigm was placed upon the shoulders of Stanford neuropsychologist Karl Pribram. In his book, Languages of the Brain, [110] Pribram has postulated a model of brain function based upon holographic experiments with light.

A hologram is a three-dimensional image of an object or scene created by the projection of an interference pattern by means of lasers. Pribram developed his neural hologram theory because it seemed to explain three major paradoxes of mental functioning. The first was the elusiveness of memory or sensory information storage in the brain. Experiments on animals have shown that if just two percent of brain tissue is left undamaged, memory function remains essentially intact.

Imagine if 98 percent of your kidneys were gone, but the other 2 percent worked so well you couldn't find anything wrong at all . . . Memory seems to be distributed throughout the brain, located in no particular part. [111]

The second paradox was that of perceptual constancy. An object, once identified, can be recognized in myriad situations and perspectives from which it was never before known. There is a

---

109. Ibid., p. 142.
110. Karl H. Pribram, Languages of the Brain (Englewood Cliffs, New Jersey: Prentice-Hall, Inc., 1971), chapter eight.
111. Karl Pribram (interview by Daniel Goleman), "Holographic Memory," "Psychology Today" February 1979, p. 72.

flexibility in perceptual identification which cannot be explained in terms of a hard-wired brain with fixed connections.

The third paradox was that of the transfer of learning. Once a motor skill is learned (e.g. writing) it can be transferred to different parts of the body which are controlled by totally separate areas of the brain. If one is right-handed one can, though with difficulty, still write with the left hand, or with one's big toe, or with a pencil between one's teeth.

> The puzzle is that the part of the brain that controls the left hand, or the teeth, or the big toe has never written anything before. How does that particular group of brain cells process information about writing? [112]

The answer to all three paradoxes can be easily understood if one assumes a holographic theory of brain functioning. Pribram further developed his model by postulating that the brain was a frequency analyzer. Not only do wavefronts create interference patterns, thus creating neural holograms, but the brain cells and sensory neurons themselves interpret information by analyzing its wave frequency. Experimental studies in auditory, somatosensory, somatomotor, and visual systems all support Pribram's hypothesis of neuronal frequency analysis. Thus the brain functions not only through electrochemical wavefronts, but interprets reality itself as a wave phenomenon. If Pribram is correct then the human brain may be making the best of a difficult situation. In a universe of relative and fluctuating wave phenomena, a holographic wave analysis may be the most accurate "reflection" of reality.

---

112. Ibid., p. 72.

A Cosmic Hologram:
The Universe as a Projection

"...the stream of knowledge is heading toward a non-mechanical reality; the universe begins to look more like a great thought than like a great machine" [113]
— *Sir James Jeans*

String theory is one possible resolution to the conflicting theories of relativity and quantum mechanics. It does away with particles and forces and simplifies (or complicates) the universe by positing a cosmic symphony of energetic, vibrating strings as the elementary constituents. But even this promising unification opens the universe to eleven hypothetical dimensions (rather than the known four); parallel universes; mass-less particles; tachyons (faster-than-light particles); rips in the fabric of space; as well as the possibility of time travel. The resolution is thus even more bizarre than the problems and dilemmas it is attempting to solve. String theory (and its more refined successor, M-theory) are so extraordinary that they are akin to science-fiction. And yet they are the most-promising, respectable avenues of current cutting-edge physics. And they support the possibility of a holographic universe.

Nobel laureate Gerard 't Hooft and co-inventor of string theory, Leonard Susskind, proposed a holographic model for the universe. The tiny strings can become immense membranes encompassing everything. According to physicist Brian Greene:

---

113. Sir James Jeans, <u>The Mysterious Universe</u> (Cambridge: Cambridge University Press, 1937), p. 122.

The laws of physics would act as the universe's laser, illuminating the real processes of the cosmos—processes taking place on a thin, distant surface—and generating the holographic illusions of daily life. [114]

Greene then concludes in a follow-up assessment:

Of all the clues discussed here, I'd pick the holographic principle as the one most likely to play a dominant role in future research. . . . That string theory naturally incorporates the holographic principle—at least in examples amenable to mathematical analysis—is another strong piece of evidence suggesting the principle's validity. I expect that regardless of where the search for the foundations of space and time may take us, regardless of modifications to string/M-theory that may be waiting for us around the bend, holography will continue to be a guiding concept. [115]

Leonard Susskind explains string theory's role in forming a cosmic hologram. In The Black Hole War he states that tiny one-dimensional strings are extremely energetic due to the uncertainty of the quantum action. They vibrate with zero point motion and can stretch out to the boundary of the known universe, encompassing it in a cosmic membrane. The information-loss dilemma that Stephen Hawking posited as a result of evaporating black holes or singularities is thus refuted. For bits of information are stored (not lost) in the strings and constitute a cosmic hologram, which is everything we know and experience: ". . . all the world is a hologram." [116]

While string/M theory may never be proven, it is mathematically elegant. Many of the greatest mathematicians and physicists are currently working out the complexity of the mathematical equations. The possibility exists it may be the universal substrate: the Theory of Everything. Susskind explains further:

Here, then, is the conclusion that 't Hooft and I had

114. Brian Greene, The Fabric of the Cosmos (New York: Alfred A. Knopf, 2004), pp. 482-3.
115. Ibid., p. 485.
116. Leonard Susskind, The Black Hole War (New York: Little, Brown and Company, 2008), p. 156.

reached: the three-dimensional world of ordinary experience—the universe filled with galaxies, stars, planets, houses, boulders, and people—is a hologram, an image of reality coded on a distant two-dimensional surface. [117]

But even the utter strangeness of complementarity is dwarfed by the bizarre Holographic Principle. It seems that the solid three-dimensional world is an illusion of a sort, the real thing taking place out at the boundaries of space. [118]

Thus the universe is possibly an objective illusion. For there are no absolute conditions. Reality may be a holographic projection formed by the interference pattern of energy. Energy may itself be a form of consciousness. Consciousness may itself be a form of energy. Relativity and quantum mechanics can be synthesized through string theory by realizing that light (as well as all wave phenomena) is merely an illusion—a tangible illusion admittedly—but an illusion nonetheless. Even Albert Einstein remarked, "Reality is merely an illusion, albeit a very persistent one." [119]

Everything is relative. The universe is in flux. Objective reality (as shown earlier in the hypothetical experiment with the two rocketships) is dependent upon the subjective state of the observer. Hence, reality not only appears to be, but actually is perspectival. Energy and light (the sole known information carrier in the universe) are thus tantamount to a subjective illusion, but an objective reality from the viewpoint of the observer, for in the realm of electromagnetic radiation appearance and reality are one. But such radiation can only manifest itself through movement. Thus motion and change are the basis of reality—the basis of our interpretation of reality—but reality is our interpretation of it.

Whether in the universal hardware itself (matter which is composed of perpetual motion atoms or strings vibrating within electron shells or energetic strings) or in the universal energy supply such as light, everything is susceptible to relativistic wave distortion. It is the nature of life. And nothing more can be done. Reality is a wave phenomenon. The human mind may be merely a frequency

---

117. Ibid., p. 298.
118. Ibid., p. 434.
119. Michie, op. cit., p. 175.

analyzer and receptor. It is a lens within the universal hologram, and it cannot see the forest for the trees.

The laws of physics are topsy-turvy. Movement can occur without the use of energy. (Light can travel forever and yet remain essentially intact.) Perpetual motion machines are considered impossible. (And yet the atom with its orbiting electrons or strings comprise an eternal system of perpetual motion—using what for energy?) The paradoxes of relativity and quantum mechanics have not yet been resolved. It appears as if the universe is a tenuous wave—a probability wave or a "tendency to exist"—a probabilistic phenomenon operating in accordance with the "uncertainty principle." The universe is hence relative and in flux. Events and fundamental properties are therefore indeterminate.

But perhaps the choice of paradigms is wrong. Perhaps the emphasis should be placed not upon tangible objects, but rather upon thoughts. Such is the contention of Professor A.D. Allen in his article on physical nature in the "Foundations of Physics." Allen speculates that the fundamental elements of the universe may not be physical entities at all, but rather the operating principles or engrams of behavior—the underlying thoughts or concepts governing the world. Even the eminent astronomer, Sir James Jeans, proposes: "It may be that each individual consciousness is a brain cell in a universal mind."[120]

Such a universal mind would be so vast and intricate that only a holographic system could incorporate its being. A virtual hologram of continuous waves merging and diverging, imprinting and conveying data throughout the whole. A process, not a goal. A force field of pure thought. A consciousness and energy which cannot die. A "real illusion" which is never the same, but which nevertheless has effect. Always growing in patterns of richness and complexity. Assimilating. Correlating. Collating. Integrating. This universe of waves may actually be a hologram—the interference patterns, the thoughts of a cosmic mind. Perhaps consciousness is itself a "living" process. Perhaps reality itself is only a dream. Or as Nobel laureate Niels Bohr states unequivocally: "Everything we call real is made of things that cannot be regarded as real." [121]

---

120. Sir James Jeans as quoted by Paul Hawker in <u>Soul Survivor</u> (Kelowna, British Columbia, Canada: Northstone Publishing Inc., 1998), p. 161.
121. Niels Bohr as quoted by Amit Goswami, <u>The Quantum Doctor</u> (Charlottesville, Virginia: Hampton Roads Publishing Company, Inc., 2004, 2011), p. X.

PART THREE

The Creation of a Dream

"...any condition ever becoming reality is first dreamed." [122]

—*Edgar Cayce*

122. Harmon H. Bro, <u>Edgar Cayce on Dreams</u> (New York: Warner Books, Inc., 1968), p. 160.

Anonymous. *Untitled engraving for Camille Flammarion.* 1888.

The Creation of Reality

"...imagination is the beginning of creation." [123]
George Bernard Shaw

The suspicion exists that life is a "real" dream, that all existence is "really" an illusion. And if all is illusion, if everything is mere dream-substance, then subjective perception and imagination are tantamount to the truth. Creativity is hence a divine power. The artist is akin to a god. Creative endeavors are thus an attempt to reformulate reality, to dream a new dream, to refashion the universe.

And God said, Let there be light and there was light. [124]

The power of thought and expression invokes a new existence. God in the role of artistic creator of the world. But man, being the most imaginative of animals, is vying with the divine and envisioning a new world, a world in his image, a world of his image. For reality is only an interaction of the mind.

If objective idealism is correct, then the universe is a collective dream. Each individual is projecting and confirming the conceptual image of others. The relevance of imagination and creativity (or in other words, art) is through the mental construction of relative subjective realities which may in fact be real. What was once considered a so-called retreat from reality may very well be the

123. George Bernard Shaw, Back to Methuselah (New York: Penguin Books, 1957), p. 70.
124. The Holy Bible (King James version) Genesis 1:3.

closest link and expression of the universal essence. The ivory-tower idealist, the childish dreamer, the artist, writer, and poet could thus be closer to the truth than their supposedly "realistic" counterparts— materialists and pragmatists who are determined by existence rather than determining it.

> "...I hear you say 'Why?' Always 'Why?' You see things; and you say 'Why?' But I dream things that never were; and I say 'Why not?'" [125]

Such is the wisdom of the serpent in Shaw's novel <u>Back to Methuselah</u>. The serpent is admonishing Adam and Eve for their unimaginative dependence on the external, for according to his Weltanschauung all existence is simply a matter of creative imagination. And when all is imagination why be obsessed with circumstantial reality? One can just as well dream another dream, subjectively envisioning thought into existence. Thus Shaw's serpent is advocating the creative conceptualization of reality.

Artistic endeavors are the first step in this idealization of reality, for the artist transforms subjective ideas into objective expressions, the internal to the external, imagination into form. The artist, in so doing, consciously engenders a new reality, a new form and meaning where previously there was none. The artist thus displays the ability to synthesize the subjective and the objective into an integrated whole. He has tapped a process which may very well be the "philosophers' stone," the alchemical key to the universe. The meaning of art and creation, perhaps the meaning of life itself, is this inherent urge to shape the world into our own dreams and ideals. Creativity and imagination are hence vital factors in altering or literally "reconceiving" the universe. The power of art may thus have been previously overlooked or ignored. Its significance lies in its ability to recreate and reconceive and then transform this new conception into physical, objective reality. It is an evolutionary attribute which distinguishes man from the animals: the ability to envision and reconstruct the components of his existence, the ability to dream his dream until it becomes real. The power is a process formerly attributed to the gods. And man himself may possess the germ of the divine, the latent power to imagine and manifest his own reality.

---

125. Shaw, <u>op. cit.</u>, p. 67.

"The mind is its own place, and in itself
Can make a heav'n of hell, a hell of heav'n..." [126]

Such is Satan's pronouncement in Milton's Paradise Lost. After he falls from grace Satan defiantly proclaims that the mind is the sole arbiter of reality—"What matter where, if I be still the same . . ."[127] —for reality is, so to speak, determined by the mind.

However the problem is that this mental determination is subject to both internal and external factors. The mind perceives the world through sensory experience or sensa which correspond to external objects of reality. But the mind also conceives and generates sensa of its own (whether spontaneously and independently or simply as a reprocessing of stored data), hence the existence of dreams, hallucinations, and other imaginative appearances. But are they mere "appearances?" The mind cannot distinguish. For whether caused externally or internally the thought is still the same. There is no difference to the undifferentiating mind, for regardless of origin all mental experience is real. Thus the blessing of creative imagination is also a disguised curse. For who is to draw the line between madness and creative genius? Who is to say that this is fantasy and this is real?

The mind thus serves as an interface between imagination and reality. It not only perceives sensory stimuli, but also creates it, and sensory stimuli are the mode through which one perceives the universe. There is no alternative. For awareness is the direct result of sensation, and so too is our consciousness of reality. But reality can only be known through sensation (whether external or internal), hence the incorporation and integration of subjective experience into reality. The mind therefore actually fabricates reality through consciousness. Life is thus tantamount to a dream or story which one makes up and dreams as one goes along. The interpretation is thus up to the individual reader or dreamer. And such an interpretation can literally drive one insane.

---

126. John Milton, Paradise Lost and Paradise Regained (New York: Airmont Publishing Company, Inc., 1968), p. 17.
127. Ibid., p. 17.

SECTION ONE

The Challenge of the Dream

Reality is an interaction. Subjective and objective combine to form a perceptual interface—a hologram of consciousness with varying degrees of clarity. Each subject projects his own fragment of the pattern. And each, in turn, is projected by the other. The result is a collage of reality perspectives each of which is an interaction of perception and manifestation. However the acknowledgment of subjective influence is not as all-promising as it might seem. For subjectivity itself is controlled by two limiting factors. The first is that each individual is determined in part by both cultural and biological conditions. Hence each subjective framework is biased and relatively resistant to change. The second factor is that each subjective framework creates its own interpretation. There is no absolute standard of reference. Thus the infinite freedom of creative imagination can also be an endless nightmare of madness. The distinction is left to individual perspective. Subjectivity can hence facilitate either creation or destruction.

The problem of limited perceptual frameworks is more complex than it seems. Most apparent is the obvious conditional nature of the senses. The human eye, for example, is sensitive to only 300 nanometers of the electromagnetic spectrum, a tiny portion of the available light. All other radiant energy is totally invisible to humans. However, many other animals are sensitive to different frequencies of electromagnetic radiation. Sidewinders, for example, can detect infrared light. At night, in total darkness, they can actually "see" the heat from the bodies of their prey. Such varying sensitivities extend to the other senses as well. Bats and dolphins can hear far beyond the auditory range of the human ear. And dogs and other mammals have a more developed sense of smell. Thus only a small portion of "reality" is capable of being known. But all this is elementary school-day facts.

What is even more restrictive than limited sensitivity is the physiological distortion of sensation. For even the stimuli which manages to pass through these sensorial "windows" becomes distorted by physiological processes within the nervous system itself. As was mentioned earlier, the lateral inhibitory process within the eye results in the illusory appearance of brightness-darkness contrasts and Mach bands. Other examples abound. There is no escaping it, for the distorting mechanisms are physically geared into perception. And what's worse, this warped stimuli goes through further distortion in the mind. The experiment on binocular perception (discussed earlier) shows conclusively that the mind itself imposes a perceptual framework which subjectively alters visual phenomena. These idealized frameworks are thus also mentally geared into perception. Hence both physical and innate mental processes necessarily distort vision.

Further complications arise through social and cultural factors. Not only are children in this culture taught to conform to the view of others, but their social training is so ingrained that even as adults they will falsify "objective" data in favor of consensus opinion. They will alter their visual interpretations in order to conform to the perception of others, even when that "reality" is clearly false. The following experiments on group pressure and conformity are cases in point.

Reality—A Social Consensus?

"In a wonderland they lie,
Dreaming as the days go by,
Dreaming as the summers die..." [128]

Conformity is the basis for man's conception of reality. Agreement is a requisite for any valid frame of reference. Man is a social animal. He needs others to tell him what is real. He needs others to confirm his own individual beliefs. Consensus is thus necessary for a feeling of security, for a feeling that one's perceptions are indeed correct. If one deviates from the norm, one's viewpoint is immediately questioned. One's framework of reality is placed in jeopardy, not only by one's peers and by society at large, but perhaps more importantly even by oneself. One has doubts, one is pressured to change, and one wants to change and conform. One feels safe among the masses, for one is no longer responsible. Others also share the same viewpoint, the same reality and beliefs. This adaptive mechanism of social consensus is clearly demonstrated in the famous autokinetic study of Muzafer Sherif. [129]

The "autokinetic effect" is the illusory shifting of a stationary point of light when viewed in a darkened room. Focusing on the light over a period of time results in muscle fatigue. This causes nystagmus

128. Lewis Carroll, Through the Looking-Glass: and what Alice found there (New York: Random House, Inc., 1946), p. 166.
129. Muzafer Sherif, The Psychology of Social Norms (New York: Harper & Row Publishers, 1936).

(a shifting or jerking in the eye muscles). Sherif observed that subjects created a subjective standard of movement when lacking an external framework for comparison. For example, without any background objects against which to measure, one subject might see the light movement to be consistently about four inches while another subject consistently sees the movement to be about twelve. "Sherif concluded that when a human being finds himself in a situation ungoverned by norms, he simply creates his own." [130]

Sherif went on to test the effects of social influence, the tendency for an individual to be affected by the beliefs and perceptions of others. Subjects were once again tested, but this time with another individual present. Both subjects were questioned about the apparent movement of the light.

> And interestingly, as the test proceeded, their responses became more and more similar. Each subject, listening to the others, adjusted his standards bit by bit until the separate standards converged into one standard. [131]

Thus the effects of social influence upon man's perception of reality actually determines that reality to a large extent. Individual differences must merge into a collective vision of truth, of consensus reality, or even consensus insanity. For who is to say that what is generally agreed upon is real.

In another experiment on social conformity Solomon Asch (1951)[132] discovered that people not only tend to agree, but will actually lie to conform with the general consensus. Even when objective measures are available, even when the general consensus is clearly wrong, one third of Asch's subjects lied simply in order to conform. The experiment was ostensibly one of visual perception. In reality it was one of social conformity.

One target subject was placed together with between four and seven other subjects who were secretly confederates of the experimenter. Their purpose was to evaluate line lengths in comparison to a standard

---

130. James F. Calhoun & Joan Ross Acocella, Psychology of Adjustment and Human Relationships (New York: Random House, Inc., 1978), p. 276.
131. Ibid., p. 276.
132. Solomon Asch, "Effects of Group Pressure upon the Modification and Distortion of Judgment" (in Groups, Leadership, and Men, H. Guetzkow (editor)) (Pittsburgh: Carnegie Press, 1951).

line. Asch wanted to test the effects of social influence upon subjects who knew that the general consensus was wrong.

As the experiment proceeded all the "confederates" suddenly falsified the correct response. The answer was obvious, and in subsequent studies by Deutsch and Gerard[133] the subjects, when asked separately and alone, almost always made the correct selection. The question was how would the target subject react in the face of unanimous disagreement even though he knows everyone else is wrong? In this and subsequent follow-up studies Asch found that about 75 percent of the subjects conformed at least once to group pressure. Repeated testing led to an expected decrease in conformity. However, out of all total responses 35 percent were still in agreement with the false judgment. In other words, over one third of the subjects repeatedly falsified their answers in order to conform with the erroneous views of others. They did not want to stand apart from the crowd.

Asch further pointed out that this one third ratio was with subjects who knew that the answer was wrong but conformed nevertheless; involved a group of strangers whom the subjects would probably never again meet; and involved a group that put no pressure on the subjects to conform. Asch reasoned that the percentage of conformance would thus be much higher if the subjects had some doubt about their judgments; involved a group whom the subjects knew and on whom they depended; and involved a group which put pressure upon the subjects to conform. Asch explains the consequences of his studies:

> May we simply conclude that (groups) can induce persons to shift their decision and convictions in almost any desired direction, that they can prompt us to call true what we yesterday deemed false, that they can make us invest the identical action with the aura of rightness or with the stigma of grotesqueness and malice?[134]

The answer is obvious. Asch and Sherif have clearly demonstrated

---

133. M. Deutsch & H.B. Gerard, "A Study of Normative and Informational Social Influence Upon Individual Judgment," Journal of Abnormal and Social Psychology, 1955, Volume 51, pp. 629-36.

134. Solomon E. Asch, "Studies of Independence and Conformity: I. A Minority of One Against a Unanimous Majority," Psychological Monographs, 70, no. 9, Whole #416 (1956), p. 2.

man's need for a consensus reality, a generally agreed upon appraisal of life. Asch furthermore showed that people will even lie, will deny their own judgments in order to conform with the group. The question is how much of this lying is actually conscious in everyday life and how much is socially ingrained, inherent in one's culture, taught and reinforced from the moment of birth. This distortion may be so much a part of the cognitive process, so much a part of one's social being, that one is no longer aware of its falseness. One takes it as true.

Thus the problem with these social pressures is that they can become so severe and widespread that they exist as an inherent aspect of one's culture. As mentioned earlier, the belief in ghosts and spirits may be affirmed in one culture while in another it is denied. Through social conditioning such perceptions will receive either positive or negative reinforcement. Which culture is right? Which perspective is true? If objective idealism is correct then both perspectives may be true. For if reality is a holographic interface then multiple interpretations can exist, each of which is as valid as the other. Light can be both wave or particle depending upon one's point of view. Ghosts may not exist in a technological society simply because their hologram is denied. But in primitive cultures, lacking the objective groundwork of science, such holographic projections may gain sufficient "light" or energy to become real. The power of belief. The religious insistence on faith. As Sherif has shown, when an objective groundwork is lacking, people are swayed severely by group consensus, even when such consensus is formed upon an illusion. For the autokinetic effect was merely the result of muscle fatigue in the eyes. And yet most subjects came to agree upon both the direction and distance of these illusory movements of light.

Thus the studies on social conformity by both Asch and Sherif point out the unreliability of the group as a reality index. There is no inherent objectivity involved in a social consensus, but simply a merging of subjective reinforcement. What passes for reality may hence be nothing more than a delusion. Social consensus, as shown by Sherif and Asch, may be just as open to suspicion as any subjective account. But when faced with a question of alliance between an individual minority view and the majority view of society, common sense would lean towards social consensus. For there is safety in numbers. But what if reality is consensus insanity What if it is all a consensus illusion, a consensus dream? We could all be wandering through the Cheshire Cat's Wonderland of madness, formed and projected by the cultural hologram in which we were born.

The effects of social influence thus determine the societally acceptable nature of reality. And this reality is relative, varies cross-culturally, and even contradicts. The social consensus reality must thus be questioned as to its credibility and viability, for while practical on the secure mundane level, such a belief system isolates one from other potentially enhancing points of view. A study on mystical experiences illustrates this deadening effect of social influence.

> In a revealing survey, pollsters Andrew Greely and William McCready discovered that two out of five Americans in a random sample had experienced at least once in their lives a mystic moment where they felt they had become completely "one" with the universe. Despite the commonness of this experience, virtually no one in their sample had ever told anyone about it before. Why? In our culture, they feared, this mystical experience would be seen as a symptom of mental illness rather than a spiritual breakthrough.[135]

Such culturally inhibiting factors not only force people to deny such experiences, but also arouse fear or embarrassment thus punishing their occurrence. Rather than encouraging, modern society devalues these feelings so that the mystical experience is being conditioned out of existence.

Social consensus is hence effectively manipulating one's reality—on a subtle, refined level through social influence—on a gross, overt level through physical abuse and imprisonment. Rosenhan's classic labeling experiment (1973)[136] showed how a simple "deviant" behavior symptom (hearing voices) is enough to acquire the malign label "schizophrenic" and get one admitted to a mental hospital. Even with subsequent normal behavior and no mention of voices, Rosenhan's eight "pseudopatients" still took an average of seventeen days before they were released back into society. What is more astonishing—not one of the staff personnel or psychiatrists detected the alleged patients to be phony, whereas nearly thirty percent of the real patients questioned or accused the pseudopatients of deception. And when the "schizophrenics" were finally released it was not with a clean bill of sanity, but rather with the tainted label "schizophrenia in

---

135. Daniel Goleman & Richard J. Davidson (editors), Consciousness (New York: Harper & Row, Publishers, Inc., 1979), p. 176.
136. David L. Rosenhan, "On Being Sane in Insane Places," Science, 179 (4070), 1973, pp. 250-258.

remission." Thus the labels of madness stuck. Even with outward behavior manifesting total normality and sanity, a single admission of "hearing voices" was enough to mark one as crazy.

But what if disembodied spirits do exist? And voices? And Joan of Arc? In today's rational society there is no room for such possibilities. Hence all future Joan of Arcs will be found in mental wards—label: paranoid schizophrenia. What better example of consensus insanity, societal pressure, and the perspectival nature of reality! Joan of Arc was considered an inspired leader, a heroine who led an army to victory. But then her "voices" and claims of speaking to God were "proven" evidence of her consorting with demons. She was burned at the stake for being a witch. Then, centuries later, Joan of Arc became Saint Joan, beatified and canonized by the very same Roman Catholic Church responsible for her murder. Could reality be so relative and whimsical? Is the universe itself merely a point-of-view?

Socrates stopped dead in his tracks and remained motionless and speechless in deep thought for an entire day—if occurring in today's suburban mall he would be carted off to the nearest asylum—label: catatonic schizophrenia. More recently, Nobel prize laureate and mathematician, John Nash (inventor of Game Theory), found himself in an asylum committed as a schizophrenic. His story is portrayed in the motion picture "A Beautiful Mind" [137] starring Russell Crowe. However, in John's case he was never "cured," but simply came to terms with and accepted his voices. Thus the mental wards may be the residence of the greatest visionaries, creative geniuses, and deep thinkers of our time. It is simply our sterile consensus viewpoint which is retarding cultural growth. Social influence is thus deadening man to alternate modes and visions of reality, literally warping one's mind to see only an agreed upon norm. All else, even if perceived, is simply rejected as untrue.

Reality is thus a matter of cultural bias, the direct effect of social influence upon one's developing beliefs. In different societies different beliefs mold one's perception of reality. Awarenesses hence alter varying with the degrees of "distortion." Perhaps the most extreme example of such cultural distortion comes from the anecdotal reports of early explorers. According to Charles Darwin and the crew of the H.M.S. Beagle, the natives of Patagonia were unable to see the ship in which they had arrived. The natives, accustomed only to small

---

137. "A Beautiful Mind," (Universal Pictures, 2001), Ron Howard (director), Akiva Goldsman (screen writer) from the 1994 book of the same title, Sylvia Nasar (author).

canoes, were unable to conceive of the existence of such large vessels. Hence, the Beagle did not exist. It could not be perceived, even when anchored only a quarter-mile off shore.[138] Or as Aldous Huxley explains: "Our normal common-sense universe is the product of a particular habit of perception—perhaps a bad habit . . ."[139]

Psychologists now know for a fact that one's previous experience with the world affects subsequent neurological filtering and programming. In other words, one's conception of reality affects one's perception of reality. Thus it is not, as was previously held, a simple matter of sensation of physical elements, but rather a dynamic, interactive process involving the mind. British psychologist R.L. Gregory explains it more succinctly: "We not only believe what we see: to some extent we see what we believe."[140] Gregory's position, which he maintains in his book aptly entitled The Intelligent Eye, is that perception is actually an interpretation of hypotheses (deduced and induced from sensory data) with which we form a mental construct of reality. And such constructs are heavily influenced by society.

However the most disturbing aspect of cultural bias is not one of mental constructs or processing, for such constructs can, however difficult, theoretically be changed. But what is distressing is that discoveries in developmental psychology show an actual physiological basis for culturally-influenced sensory distortion. In other words, what is disturbing is not that others influence one's perception of reality, but that on a very "real" physical basis one is literally forced to succumb. One can see reality no differently than what was culturally and environmentally ingrained. And this is perhaps the most unsettling framework—a view of reality from which one cannot escape. The distorting mechanism responsible is that of the developmental plasticity of the nervous system.

Developmental plasticity is the ability of the nervous system to functionally adapt itself to the environment. During the early stages of an organism's growth, cortical structures have not yet been fully geared to corresponding functions. At certain critical periods (varying with different functions) such structures are susceptible to modification in order to optimally adapt the organism to the environment. And yet environments differ in their demands and

---

138. Lawrence LeShan, Alternate Realities (New York: Ballantine Books, 1976), pp. 6-7.

139. Robert S. Baker and James Sexton, Aldous Huxley: Complete Essays (Chicago: Ivan R. Dee, Publisher, 2000), Volume II, p. 384. From "Pascal."

140.Richard L. Gregory, The Intelligent Eye (New York: McGraw-Hill Book Company, 1970), p. 15.

pressures. And an environment composed of certain stresses or deprivations can result in the development of a sensory system maladaptive to another environment. The following experimental studies on visual developmental plasticity are cases in point.

Developmental Plasticity
in the Visual System:
The Effects of a Carpentered World

The classic experiment on kittens by Colin Blakemore et. al. (1974)[141] showed the existence of orientation neurons in the visual cortex. Not only were the existence of such neurons made physically evident, but also their modifiability during critical periods of development. What Blakemore showed was that visual acuity for orientations was affected by early visual stimulation in the developing organism's environment.

Blakemore raised kittens in a visual environment consisting solely of either vertical or horizontal stripes as a background. After exposure during the critical period (4-6 weeks) kittens reared with vertical stimulation showed visual acuity for orientations only within 45 degrees of the vertical. Kittens reared with horizontal stimulation showed visual acuity for orientations only within 45 degrees of the horizontal. In both cases visual acuity for obliques and opposed 90 degree angles was lost. While it is impossible to say just what the kittens did or did not subjectively see when exposed to such angles, the fact remains that they were functionally blind to orientations not within 45 degrees of their original critical-period stimulation. Thus early environmental factors can result in severe sensory distortion.

Anatomical studies indicate that this sensory distortion penetrates right down to cortical structures. Hubel and Wiesel (1979)[142] showed that these orientation neurons are grouped together in orientation columns. Furthermore, they found the columns for such blind angles

141. Colin Blakemore and Richard C. Van Sluyters, "Experimental Analysis of Amblyopia and Strabismus," British Journal of Ophthalmology, 1974, Volume 58, pp. 176-181.
142. David H. Hubel and Torsten N. Wiesel, "Brain Mechanisms of Vision," Scientific American, 1979, Volume 241, pp. 150-162.

to be no longer functional. The feature detectors for non-stimulated orientations had been lost. While there is some evidence for partial recovery, the effect appears long-lasting and more or less permanent. Thus meridional amblyopia (loss of acuity for certain angles) has been shown capable of being induced in kittens solely as a result of early visual experience. The question now is whether or not such visual developmental plasticity occurs in humans.

The problem of similar research on humans is apparent. No scientist can ethically conduct such drastic experiments on human beings, nor can he provide such rigorous controls. Hence the development of human sensory systems can only be inferred or generalized from that of animals. This is the reason why cross-cultural studies are so weak. There are not enough controls to insure that the results obtained are due purely to the experimental premise. Nevertheless the findings of such cross-cultural studies do show remarkable parallels to those of animals. The experiment on visual acuity to orientations in Cree Indians is a case in point.

Frost and Annis (1973)[143] tested the visual acuity for orientations in a group of Euro-Canadian university students in contrast to a group of Cree Indians. What they found in optical-tilt experiments was that the Euro-Canadians showed greater acuity for horizontal-vertical orientations in comparison to oblique orientations, whereas the Cree Indians showed no such differentiation. The Euro-Canadian group was suffering the visual impairment of a modern, "carpentered" world with all its straight lines and perpendicular structures. They were not perceiving the world as it really exists. Frost and Annis explain the differences as the result of early exposure to a visual environment. In the Euro-Canadian group the 90 degree angular environment resulted in loss of visual acuity for obliques. The Cree Indian group, on the other hand, living in an "uncarpentered" natural environment suffered no such bias in the development of their visual systems.

Such cross-cultural evidence, however, is debatable. No controls or comparisons were made to insure that the effect was not genetic or else the result of educational differences. However, further evidence of possible developmental plasticity in the visual system comes from a cross-cultural study on Zambian citizens by Ahluwalia (1978). Such a study ruled out the possible genetic effects, for the experiment was between Zambians raised in urban and rural environments. The educational factor was also minimized.

---

143. Robert C. Annis and Barrie Frost, "Human Visual Ecology and Orientation Anisotrophies in Acuity," Science, 1973, Volume 182, pp. 729-731.

For this study actual susceptibility to optical illusions was measured. One was the Muller-Lyer illusion, the other was Delboeuf's illusion. Both are theoretical measures of angular-orientation preferences and hence apply to the "carpentered world" hypothesis. Ahluwalia's results are summarized by J.B. Deregowski in his book, Illusions, Patterns, and Pictures: A Cross-Cultural Perspective : "... the two groups were found to differ greatly in their illusion scores, the rural populations being, as expected, less prone to the illusion."[144] However, Deregowski goes on to conclude that cross-cultural studies on susceptibility to illusions are ambiguous and contradictory. Much is not known about genetic factors and hence such factors are not controlled. And yet, notwithstanding such objections, there is still found to be major differences in illusion scores.

> There is only one reasonably firm conclusion which the data proffer: there are cross-cultural differences in proneness to illusions and hence in the manner in which the perceptual mechanisms operate, among cultures. [145]

While the results of cross-cultural studies are in themselves weak, they do become more credible when augmented by comparative studies on animals. Together they provide a body of convincing evidence— evidence which indicates a more or less developmental plasticity in the visual system. Such plasticity results in the physiological molding of perceptual frameworks. They are frameworks which are culturally relative. They are frameworks from which one cannot escape.

---

144. J.B. Deregowski, Illusions, Patterns, and Pictures: A Cross-Cultural Perspective (New York: Academic Press, Inc., 1980), p. 45.
145. Ibid., p. 50.

The Power of Conception
Madness vs. Creative Escape

The very nature of one's subjective condition results in limited perceptual frameworks. These frameworks are determined not only by one's biological nature and social pressures, but also by early neural imprinting within the brain. Perceptual mechanisms have been more or less set since early childhood. There is no other way for one to perceive the universe. The problem is further complicated by each individual's own interpretation of the sensory data. In other words, not only are sensa filtered through one's neuronal network, but once this information is received, it is susceptible to even further modification through one's system of beliefs. Thus there is no absolute standard of reference, for each subjective framework creates its own interpretation. And who is to say which interpretation is true?

What is even more disturbing is the brain's ability to manipulate and fool its own mind. (Talk about self-deception!—This is the epitomy of the act.) Experiments on split-brain patients by psychologist Michael Gazzaniga and others show we cannot even believe what we tell ourselves. In split-brain subjects the right and left hemisphere can no longer communicate since the corpus collosum has been severed. It is as though they have two separate minds. When instructions are given to the right brain to wave or laugh, the subject obeys. When asked why they did so, the left brain which controls speech has no explanation (because it did not receive the instructions). Yet nevertheless it confabulates a reason from a plausible scenario: "the patient said he'd waved because he'd thought he'd seen someone he knew...the patient said he'd laughed because the researchers were funny." [146]

---

146. Mlodinow, op. cit., p. 190.

If the disconnected left brain were really so reasonable and rational, it would say honestly: "I'm not sure. I don't know why I waved and laughed." But instead it invents a reason for its behavior, for otherwise it would look foolish. Similarly, when the right hemisphere of a female subject is shown a nude photo, she smiles and chuckles. When asked why, her left hemisphere responds: "...oh—that funny machine." [147]

The lesson is clear and disturbing: when the rational left hemisphere needs an explanation, it concocts one. The ramifications are profound. Is belief in God and religion simply a confabulation? Are beliefs, values, and meaning simply a facile invention? While admittedly, most people have not had a commisurotomy and become split-brain patients, still, what does this say about the rational left hemisphere's tendency to invent its own reality: when unable to provide a rationale we simply confabulate! And what about science? And modern man's understanding of life? Are these all possibly just another fictional concoction? As the saying goes, "If God didn't exist, man would have to invent him."

However unsettling, this subjective filtering and interpretation of data may paradoxically provide its own solution to the dilemma. The limitation of a subjective framework, the impositions of a psychophysical set can be overcome simply by means of thought. In other words, one can imagine and interpret reality to such an extent that it will change. One can thus circumvent one's inherent limitations by simply creating an alternate perceptual set. Such is the process of creative imagination, the dream-like element of objective idealism. For one can, to a large degree, mold one's conception of reality—and reality, to a large degree, can in turn be molded by thought.

Although this may sound like New-Age gibberish, one must remember that New-Age physics lends credence to these views. Choosing, even after-the-fact, between one slit or two in the double-slit experiment, determines and alters the reality of an interference or scatter-pattern.

Hence it is possible to imaginatively transcend the limits of subjective frameworks. One is free to explore reality through the myriad vicissitudes of thought. The only problem is that this imaginative escape knows no bounds. Without a frame of reference, no matter how relative or limiting, one may eventually be unable to

---

147. Michael S. Gazzaniga, "The Split Brain in Man" from <u>Altered States of Awareness: Readings from Scientific American</u> (San Francisco: W.H. Freeman and Company, 1967), p. 124.

differentiate one's perceptions. One may become lost in a virtual wonderland of madness. And yet this is the very challenge of dream-reality: confronting and controlling the creative powers of the mind.

Such is the theme of Miguel de Unamuno's story "The Madness of Doctor Montarco." Unamuno is playing with the age-old association of madness and creative genius. His central character, Doctor Montarco, believes that the tentative imaginative side of reality is what is essential. It is the dynamic, playful, fantastic element—or in other words, the madness—which is the vitalizing power behind man's existence. Madness, in Montarco's view, is thus an integral part of life—the suppression of which will thus also suppress real life.

Montarco, a practicing physician, expresses this madness by writing fantastic stories as a sideline. It is a healthy release of "creative insanity." But this darker side of Montarco is the side of human nature which people distrust. For they lack the power to handle or express it within themselves, and so they suppress such tendencies as well as condemn its appearance in others. And thus, when Montarco begins exhibiting this "madness," they try and succeed in suppressing it in him. His patients begin deserting him; he loses his means of livelihood; his publishers eventually abandon his works; and Montarco, lacking a creative outlet, is finally "really" driven mad.

But this is after all what Montarco himself had expected. He knew he was treading on unstable ground. It was part of his philosophy of "all or nothing." One must take the risk of madness in order to transcend one's inherent limitations.

> 'You will be as gods!': thus it was the Devil tempted
> our first parents, they say. Whoever doesn't aspire
> to be more than he is, will not be anything. All or
> nothing! There is profound meaning in that. [148]

By gambling one's sanity one can playfully experiment with reality. It is the transcendental aspect of madness—the longing for another world. It is a longing which is actually "an appetite for the divine." [149] Success is simply a matter of correlating the madness into a meaningful whole, of balancing the rational and the irrational, of tempting the darkness into the light. Montarco failed, but at least he tried.

Thus the power of the dream, the creative unconscious, its very

---

148. Miguel de Unamuno, <u>Abel Sanchez and Other Stories</u> (South Bend, Indiana: Gateway Editions, Ltd., 1956), p. 189.
149. <u>Ibid.</u>, p. 189.

virtue of being boundless and unlimited in scope, produces a tentative and unstable perceptual framework, a framework which, in its extreme, is akin to madness. Freud himself recognized this affinity with respect to dreams:

> A dream, then, is a psychosis, with all the absurdities, delusions and illusions of a psychosis. A psychosis of short duration, no doubt, harmless, even entrusted with a useful function, introduced with the subject's consent and terminated by an act of his will. None the less it is a psychosis...[150]

It is an hallucinatory dissociation from reality. It is a process through which one can escape the confines of the "real."

Through dreams and creativity one can overcome the limitations of the senses. With thought and imagination one can transcend one's psychophysical set—one's mental and biological nature, social and cultural conditioning, and even one's neural imprinting in the brain. It is simply a matter of creativity, faith, and belief—a reorganization of one's system of thought. The only problem is that this avenue of escape is an "all or nothing" approach. One must take the leap of imagination to find more fertile ground. But no one knows where this leap will eventually land, whether or not one will lose one's balance and fall.

Psychotherapist Paul Stern based his "Realness Therapy" upon this dynamic nature of imagination and the unconscious. In his book, In Praise of Madness, Stern claims that madness is natural to the human psyche. For most people it is simply released through the natural process of dreaming. It is only when one becomes unbalanced that it is manifested in a full-blown psychosis, and even then it is simply a release of pent-up and suppressed feelings. According to Stern, both madness and dreams are the results of hidden and denied perspectives or "selves" allowing themselves expression. And thus they add to one's psyche a sense of wholeness and creative insight.

> This haunting but often elusive unreality is, at bottom, nothing but a reality, or potentiality, which was denied. At the time it first occurred, this denial was often an act of self-preservation. But for the

---

150. Sigmund Freud, An Outline of Psycho-Analysis (New York: W.N. Norton & Company, Inc., 1969), p. 29.

person to become himself or—which is the same—to seize his own reality, he must exorcise his ghosts by embracing them. He must appropriate the reality of his unreality. [151]

Thus, in Stern's view, it is a matter of "creative madness or insanity." Man must confront and accept the manifestations of his inner self. He must become creatively aware of the madness and reality within, if only in order to more consciously control the projected reality without. The only problem is that this inner power is awesome. To control it one must literally "be as gods." And how many are strong enough or even have the desire to become gods?

---

151. Paul J. Stern, <u>In Praise of Madness</u> (New York: Dell Publishing Co., Inc., 1972), p. 9.

SECTION TWO

Harnessing the Dream

"Our life is no Dream, but it may and will perhaps become one." [152]

—*Novalis*

152. Novalis as quoted by Thomas Carlyle in <u>Voltaire and Novalis</u> (New York: United States Book Company, 1889), p. 117.

The Philosophers' Stone
Realization of the Dream

"The things we see," Pistorius said softly, "are the
same things that are within us. There is no reality
except the one contained within us. That is why so
many people live such an unreal life. They take the
images outside them for reality and never allow the
world within to assert itself..." [153]

Nobel prize laureate, Hermann Hesse, in his novel <u>Demian</u>, is
implying that the meaning of life lies in the liberation of this creative
(and sometimes destructive) unconscious. Man denies the inner
reality, which is the only true reality, and lives his life by the dictates
of the external. Such an attempt is futile, for the creative unconscious
cannot be repressed for long, but will blossom forth and erupt into the
manifest consciousness of the world. The darkness of the unknown
must ultimately see the light.

The process is evolutionary. Only the advanced can harness the
creative insanity. But this madness is inherent to all mankind. This
godlike ability lies dormant and repressed within the subconscious.
Through dreams it subtly manifests into the awareness of the
receptive. Those who recognize its existence consequently tap the
flow of energy, thus gaining the power of intuitive insight and creative
expression. But the power is latent within all men, for all men can
imagine, and all men can dream. This fact has been established in sleep
laboratories throughout the world. Until recently it was impossible to
scientifically observe the subjective process of dreaming. However,

---

153. Hermann Hesse, <u>Demian</u> (New York: Harper & Row Publishers, Inc., 1965),
p. 96.

Aserinsky's discovery of REM periods concurrent with dreaming made it possible to detect the dream while in progress. Even self-professed non-dreamers who were awakened during REM surprisingly acknowledged that they were indeed dreaming. Psychologists thus concluded that it was not an inability to dream that was in question, but rather an inability to recall the dream—a psychological repression and denial, as it were. Experimental sleep research hence proved that everyone dreams whether or not they remember the experience.

Further research indicates that the mind is not a passive recipient of sensory stimuli. Rather, it is an active anticipatory function which will degenerate without meaningful stimulation. This is not some vague epistemological theory dealing with speculative concepts, but an actual physiological process supported by tangible facts. Experiments in sensory deprivation have conclusively dismissed the theory of the mind as a homeostatic process. Rather than being aroused by stimulation, processing the information, and then returning to a homeostatic state of balance, the mind apparently seeks out stimulation and, if deprived of meaningful sensations (as in sensory deprivation experiments), will begin to malfunction and eventually create stimulation of its own. The internally generated stimulation can take the form of hallucinations, delusions, or a combination of both in what is described as "waking dreams."

Subjects may see lights and images, hear sounds and voices, believe themselves dreaming when EEG monitoring shows them to be awake. In extreme cases they may even become paranoid and panic-stricken as delusions of persecution or unfounded fear (e.g. that the building is burning down or that they are being driven insane) force them to terminate the experiment before completion. Thus the physiological mechanism of the mind actively engages the perception of reality. Denied this stimulation from the external, the mind will produce internal sensa of its own, creating its own inner world of subjective reality.

Electroencephalographic readings indicate that this breakdown of conscious functioning accompanied by a consequent flare-up of imagination is akin to a gradual emergence of the unconscious. Numerous studies on extended periods of deprivation show an increasing tendency toward sleep-like patterns and slower frequencies in the alpha range with time (i.e. the longer the period of sensory deprivation, the more the EEG patterns resemble sleep, relaxed awareness, or trance).[154] This is apparently the result of dissociation

154. Duane Schultz, Sensory Restriction (New York: Academic Press, Inc., 1965), pp. 35-42.

from external reality, followed by a release of unconscious imagery and thought. Indeed, as the experiment continues, subjects find it increasingly difficult to distinguish reality from dreams, for to the mind all mental experience is real. Thus when external stimulation is absent, the mind begins stimulating and reacting to itself, imagining and creating its own inner world.

But this reality generated by the creative unconscious is often of a distorted and frightening nature. Apparently, when forced to envision and sustain a reality of their own, most people prove unequal to the task. It seems man does not wish to be an artistic creator, but merely a passive audience to a world already in existence. Man does not desire a world of his making. Hence the result of being forced to confront one's inner self, to create a reality of one's own, is a breakdown of reality processing, possible fear and/or delusions, and eventually widespread cortical malfunction.

Subjects undergoing sensory deprivation for two to three days reported feeling dazed and confused along with an inability to concentrate.

> Consequently, they lapsed into daydreaming, gave up efforts at organized thinking, and allowed their minds to wander. A few subjects experienced "blank periods," during which they were unable to think of anything at all. [155]

Obviously total subjectivity is a negative condition for those lacking the courage of creative imagination. For without external distractions, the conscious mind loses control, becomes disoriented and unable to function properly, and is slowly invaded and overrun by subconscious or unconscious processes. Through hallucinations, delusions, and dream-like states, the unconscious seemingly flares up and overwhelms the undisciplined mind. Thus man must strengthen his will to harness the full potential of the unconscious. Rather than being allowed to run rampant, its creative power must be controlled and adapted for constructive purposes.

And yet only those strong enough can grapple with the evolutionary force of the unconscious. For those too weak—mental, emotional, and physiological degeneration will necessarily occur. Indeed, during the Korean war, sensory deprivation was used by the North Koreans

---

155. Charles A. Brownfield, The Brain Benders (New York: Exposition Press, 1972), p. 100.

to psychologically destroy their prisoners. The process, popularly known as "brainwashing," was employed to extract information, obtain written and public confessions (both true and untrue), cause incidents of treason, and instigate dissension and mutual suspicion among fellow prisoners.

The effectiveness of brainwashing was alarmingly high. Breakdown of psychological defenses caused a consequent deterioration of morale. In fact, there was a higher mortality rate (four out of ten) of prisoners dying from non-physical causes than at any other time in recorded military history.[156] The success of brainwashing was due to the weakened state of the mind after sensory deprivation, followed with subsequent propaganda (or a filling of the void).

Controlled experiments have shown that subjects do indeed become more susceptible to propaganda after extended periods of isolation.[157] The reality structure of the individual slowly begins to collapse as reinforcement from the external world is discontinued. Subjects (or prisoners) no longer know what is real. They cannot distinguish between reality and dream, and consequently can be manipulated into believing almost anything. Any information or sensory input will be cherished and savored, for the mind deprived of stimulation will crave almost any form of sensation. In fact, according to psychologists Leuba (1955) and Dember (1960), even pain can be enjoyable under conditions of minimal stimulation![158]

Thus, only the strong and creative can profit from an enforced confrontation with the inner self. For as Fiske concludes in his article "Effects of Monotonous and Restricted Stimulation": "Unless the subject's thoughts and imagery have considerable impact, his activation level necessarily declines."[159] Peter Suedfeld further emphasizes the role played by individual character factors, particularly those involved in coping with the inner self. In his article, "Social Isolation: A Case for Interdisciplinary Research," Suedfeld examines the widely varying responses of subjects to isolation. Referring to the work of E.A. Haggard (1964) and T.I. Myers (1969), Suedfeld explains:

---

156. Ibid., p. 86.

157. T. Scott, W.H. Bexton, W. Heron, & B.K. Doane, "Cognitive Effects of Perceptual Isolation," Canadian Journal of Psychology, 1959, Volume 13, pp. 200-209.

158. Schultz, op. cit., p. 28.

159. Donald W. Fiske & Salvatore R. Maddi (Eds.), Functions of Varied Experience (Homewood, Illinois: The Dorsey Press, Inc., 1961), p. 140.

It may be noted here that the optimal adjustment to isolation and to sensory deprivation is apparently made by those subjects who are able to relax and enjoy the flow of fantasy and other primary process material which apparently cannot be efficiently warded off in these situations. [160]

In other words, those frightened or unsure of their own internal thoughts and feelings tend to be maladaptive. They either panic or suffer the ill effects of sensory deprivation.

Colin Wilson, in his philosophical spy-thriller The Black Room, builds these ideas into the major theme of his novel. The story concerns a spy network that is striving for world domination. Their greatest mind-control weapon, "the black room" or isolation chamber, is capable of "cracking" and converting even the most disciplined of agents. A rush to develop methods of combating the black room consequently ensues. It is soon discovered that highly creative individuals are capable of withstanding sensory deprivation for greater periods of time. Hence the emergence of the main character, a famous musician who gradually develops into a superman prototype with subsequent black-room experience and training.

According to Wilson, only those creatively endowed are capable of enduring and even flourishing under the rigors of sensory deprivation. For they are the only ones strong enough to envision and sustain their own inner reality. Rather than depending on the external world to provide reality indices, such creators can easily rely upon the internal creative faculty. This faculty, concludes Wilson, is the future evolutionary course of the human race—development of the creative imagination.

"The individual who has experienced solitude will not easily become a victim of mass suggestion." [161]
— Albert Einstein

160. Daniel Goleman & Richard J. Davidson (Eds.), Consciousness: Brain, States of Awareness, and Mysticism (New York: Harper & Row, Publishers, Inc., 1979), p. 162.
161. Albert Einstein quoted by Paul Hawker, Soul Survivor (Kelowna, British Columbia, Canada: Northstone Publishing Inc., 1998), p. 164.

The Lucid Dream
Metaphysical Proving Ground of the Soul

"When we dream that we are dreaming the moment of awakening is at hand." [162]

—*Novalis*

We find ourselves alone within a reality of our own creation. And yet we have no idea of who we ourselves really are. We drift from scene to scene vulnerable to any whimsical manifestation. And yet we ourselves are the sole projector of the illusion. It is a dream. It has no verifiable reality. And yet its impression is nevertheless just as subjectively real as waking life. We can cry, fall in love, become sick, hate and murder. And the phenomenon is just as meaningful as so-called "real" life. The dream is real. It is invaluable. It is a training ground for gods.

Everyone can dream, and all normal people do, but although they do, few have tapped the creative insanity of the dream, the godlike madness of unbounded imagination. Those few who have dared to dabble in this alchemical wonderland have returned with creations that have transformed the world. Not simply poems or scientific insights or intuitive understanding. But strange modes of thought which have literally revolutionized mankind.

---

162. Novalis, "Miscellaneous Observations" Fragment 16 quoted in <u>Race, Identity and Representation in Education</u> (second edition) (New York: Routledge—Taylor & Francis Group LLC, 2005), p. 129. Edited by Cameron McCarthy, Warren Crichlow, Greg Dimitriadis, and Nadine Dolby.

> In the month of November, 1619, Descartes went
> into retirement in winter quarters near Ulm . . .
> The beginning of his retirement was marked by an
> extraordinary occurrence . . . The tenth of November
> 1619, he was filled with Enthusiasm, he discovered
> the foundations of the Admirable Science, and at
> the same time his vocation was revealed to him in a
> dream. [163]

Apparently Descartes' vision is revealed in three dreams. The first
is that of a whirlwind through which Descartes struggles on his way
to church. In the second he is awakened with terror by a thunderous
outburst and a shower of sparks. The third and most important dream
is that of a dictionary opened to the words of Ausonius in Latin: 'What
path shall I follow in life?' A stranger then hands Descartes a piece
of paper and the words "Est et Non" (the Yes and No of Pythagoras)
stand out clearly in his mind.

René Descartes, French philosopher and mathematician, Father
of Modern Philosophy and Reason. His ideas have altered man's
conception of both himself and the universe. They have influenced the
intellectual course of the human race. And yet, ironically enough, this
rational philosophy stemmed from a series of three fanciful dreams.
Descartes was enamored by the dreams, proceeded to interpret them
in detail, and consequently resolved to go on and reconceive the world.

> Let us remember above all that the meditations which
> followed the dream (November 1619 to March 1620)
> are at the very source of all Cartesian philosophy, and
> that Descartes held the dream itself to be an event so
> decisive that he believed it "the most important thing
> in his life . . ." [164]

Thus on the night of November 10, 1619 the foundations of
rational thought were cast for the next four centuries, and cast as it
were literally from a foundation of dreams.

The dream has consequently, in a profound and tangible way,
successfully reconstructed man's basis of knowledge. But the dream
can effect changes in an even more refined manner, by creatively

---

163. Jacques Maritain, <u>The Dream of Descartes</u> (Port Washington, New York:
Kennikat Press, 1969), p. 13.
164. <u>Ibid.</u>, p. 21.

transforming one's inner self. The problem is that man is not yet strong enough to harness such powers. He has not yet learned to assume responsibility for his dreams, just as he has not yet learned to assume responsibility for his life. Indeed, how can one expect to control one's life when one is not even able to control one's dreams?—something that we ourselves have created and for which we ourselves are responsible.

The problem is that while dreams are a dynamo of knowledge and creativity it takes an exceptionally powerful individual to explore its depths. The rest of humanity, the mere "glib" dreamers, simply glide about the surface of the creative unconscious. They dare not penetrate the darkness of their souls, the madness of a world composed solely of thought. Hence they are controlled by the dream, by their own meaningless, incoherent, and unstructured thought, rather than bearing the responsibility of imaginative control.

Indeed, whether asleep or awake, most people are unable to control their minds. They are dominated by external factors, rather than commanding with their inner self. They allow other people and other conditions to, in effect, live their own lives. And if life is a dream, then they allow others to live their dreams. Rather than creating their own dream and living it to the fullest, they dream other people's dreams which can often turn into nightmares.

P.D. Ouspensky, the Russian mystic and philosopher, maintains that this lack of awareness and control is responsible for all our problems. According to Ouspensky, normal consciousness is akin to a dream where man is powerless to affect or understand his condition.

> . . . the state in which we are now, that is in which we work, talk, imagine ourselves conscious beings, and so forth, we often call <u>waking consciousness</u> or <u>clear consciousness</u>, but really it should be called "waking sleep" . . . All the absurdities and all the contradictions of people, and of human life in general, become explained when we realize that people <u>live in sleep</u>, do everything in sleep, and do not know that they <u>are asleep</u>.[165]

This explains why the omnipotent dream world appears so meaningless and disordered, for how can anyone be expected to be aware in their dreams when they aren't even aware in waking life.

165. P.D. Ouspensky, <u>The Psychology of Man's Possible Evolution</u> (New York: Random House, Inc., 1973), pp. 32-33.

The chaos, the boredom, the anxiety, and the madness are all simply
a reflection of their own haphazard and meaningless lives. Thus to
most people the dream is of no value or consequence, but simply an
idle pastime of their idle minds.

And yet for some people it is essential. For some the dream holds
the key to creatively synthesizing the universe. It is the philosophers'
stone and a metaphysical training ground of the soul. Awareness and
will power are the only requisites for creative dreaming. And yet it is
these very qualities which most people lack. But once they are attained
and mastered, one can essentially become a god. For in dreams one
can imaginatively create the reality one chooses. One can experiment
with a universe of one's own projection, altering and manipulating to
suit one's taste. Not just with the objects of the dream world, but
with the dream world's very essence. The metaphysical nature of the
dream is thus vulnerable to change.

The problem is in maintaining consciousness and identity while
dreaming. Being awake while dreaming does not naturally coincide,
for they are seemingly contradictory states. And yet such paradoxical
states can and do occur, but only in rare individuals such as Descartes.

On the night of November 10, 1619 Descartes' reconception
of the cosmos was inspired by three dreams. The first two dreams
were strange, but not extraordinary. However in the third and final
revelatory dream an unprecedented condition arises. Descartes
realizes that he is dreaming and begins interpreting the dream while
still asleep!

It is no surprise that a self-conscious dream changed the intellectual
history of mankind. What more appropriate vehicle of transmission
for a rationalist thinker, the father of modern philosophy? But other
individuals have also had such self-conscious or "lucid" dreams, among
them the physicist Ernst Mach, the occultist and spiritualist Oliver
Fox, the Dutch physician Frederik van Eeden, and P.D. Ouspensky
who claimed that he always dreamt "lucidly." In his paper, "A Study of
Dreams," Frederik van Eeden describes the power of lucid dreaming.

> On Sept. 9, 1904 I dreamt that I stood at a table
> before a window. On the table were different objects.
> I was perfectly well aware that I was dreaming and I
> considered what sorts of experiments I could make.
> I began by trying to break glass, by beating it with
> a stone. I put a small tablet of glass on two stones
> and struck it with another stone. Yet it would not
> break. Then I took a fine claret-glass from the table

and struck it with my fist, with all my might, at the same time reflecting how dangerous it would be to do this in waking life; yet the glass remained whole. But lo! when I looked at it again after some time, it was broken. It broke all right, but a little too late, like an actor who misses his cue. This gave me a very curious impression of being in a fake-world, cleverly imitated, but with small failures. I took the broken glass and threw it out of the window, in order to observe whether I could hear the tinkling. I heard the noise all right and I even saw two dogs run away from it quite naturally. I thought what good imitation this comedy-world was. Then I saw a decanter with claret and tasted it, and noted with perfect clearness of mind: "Well, we can also have voluntary impressions of taste in this dream-world; this has quite the taste of wine." [166]

This may all seem like New-Age gibberish and hocus-pocus. But the validity of lucid dreaming has been well-established. Sleep laboratory experiments by Stephen LaBerge at Stanford University (1979)[167] have proven beyond doubt that lucid dreaming is real. Subjects were monitored both by EEG (brain waves) and EOG (electro-oculogram: eyes movements). Prearranged signals (shifting eyes horizontally from left to right a designated number of times) indicated from the dreamer, inside the dream, to the scientists in the sleep lab, that the dreamer was lucid. EEG showed the dreamer to be in REM sleep. When awakened, the dreamer described having a lucid dream.

Experiments by Keith Hearne in England (1975)[168 & 169] also confirmed the reality of lucid dreaming. The methodology of these experiments was so convincing, that it is now widely accepted by psychologists. Lucid dreaming is a valid state of conscious awareness.

---

166. Charles Tart (editor), Altered States of Consciousness (Garden City, New York: Doubleday & Company, Inc., 1972), p. 154.
167. Stephen P. LaBerge, "Lucid Dreaming" in Psychology Today (New York: Ziff-Davis Publishing Company, January 1980), vol. 15, no. 1, pp. 48-57.
168. Ruth Mehrtens Galvin, "Control of Dreams may be Possible for a Reasonable Few" in Smithsonian (Washington, D.C.: Smithsonian Institution, August 1982), volume 13, number 5, pp. 102-104.
169. Stephen LaBerge, Lucid Dreaming (Los Angeles: Jeremy P. Tarcher, Inc., 1985), pp. 69-70.

Apparently one can consciously explore the world of dreams, metaphysically investigating the nature of subconscious reality. One can become a godlike entity, a free-flowing agent through the solipsistic universe of the mind. It is the key to spiritual advancement, enlightenment through dreams. In fact, Tibetan Buddhism, which considers life a mere dream, has as one of its spiritual practices a "yoga of dreams."[170]

The aim of this discipline is to maintain consciousness while falling asleep. In this way one can attain ultimate awareness of reality by, ironically enough, gaining ultimate awareness of the dream. As one grows more aware of the illusion of the nocturnal dream (so the philosophy goes) one will consequently grow more aware of the illusion of the daytime dream of life. In his introduction to Altered States of Consciousness Charles Tart ponders this paradoxical notion of dream-reality, the metaphysical ramifications of the lucid dream.

> Whenever I speak on the topic of dreams, I mention a very unusual sort of dream, the "lucid" dream . . . in which the dreamer knows he is dreaming and feels fully conscious in the dream itself. After discussing some of the philosophical and semantic difficulties in defining states of consciousness, I always ask whether anyone has the slightest doubt that he is awake, that is, in a "normal" state of consciousness at that moment; I have never found anyone who had difficulty in making this distinction.[171]

But what if one isn't awake? What if life is a dream as Tibetan Buddhism maintains? If objective idealism is correct then the universe is an interaction between subjective perception and objective manifestation. As such, the more powerful the individual's consciousness, the higher the degree to which he affects objective reality. Indeed, P.D. Ouspensky noted an aspect of lucid dreaming that curiously parallels the quantum physicist's problem of observer-interaction. According to Ouspensky:

> I wanted to verify a rather fantastic idea of my own which had made its appearance almost in

170. W.Y. Evans-Wentz (editor), Tibetan Yoga and Secret Doctrines (London: Oxford University Press, 1967), pp. 215-223.
171. Tart, op. cit., p. 1.

my childhood: <u>was it not possible to preserve</u> <u>consciousness in dreams</u>, that is, to know while dreaming that one is asleep and <u>to think consciously</u> as we think when awake. The first, that is, writing down dreams and so on, very soon brought me to the understanding of the impossibility of a practical realization of the usually recommended methods of observing dreams. <u>Dreams do not stand observation;</u> <u>observations change them.</u> And I very soon noticed that I was observing, not those dreams which I used to have before, but new dreams <u>which were created</u> <u>by the very fact of observation.</u> [172]

And thus, just as the observations of a physicist determine the nature of what is being observed, so too the consciousness of the lucid dreamer determines the nature of his dream. The lucid dream and the quantum universe are hence very much of the same nature.

But what then of lucid dreaming? In an objective-idealistic universe could not such lucid dreams be real? Perhaps agonizingly real? If it is all relative and intertwining? If the most powerful consciousness can make dreams real? And madness? And nightmares? Could they also be real?

In The Blind Owl, an obscure work by the Persian writer Sadegh Hedayat, the possible destructiveness of lucid dreaming is dramatized to its fullest. According to the novel's structure (and not the novel's content itself) life is an endless nightmare from which one cannot escape: "like a man dreaming, who knows that he is dreaming and wishes to awake but cannot."[173] The narrator, an eccentric dope fiend, slips continually between waking life, fantasies, drugged hallucinations, lucid dreaming, and nightmares. The result is a realization of the tenuous quality of consciousness—a consciousness which is responsible for subjectively ordering the world. Hence the narrator literally loses his mind within the solipsistic labyrinth of subjective reality (which is, according to the novel's structure, tantamount to objective reality). For he realizes that it is only thought which is real. "Life is nothing but a fiction, a mere story."[174]

The novel is thus an apology for the philosophy of idealism.

---

172. P.D. Ouspensky, <u>A New Model of the Universe</u> (New York: Random House, Inc., 1971), p. 243.
173. Sadegh Hedayat, <u>The Blind Owl</u> (London: Pan Books Ltd., 1973), p. 16.
174. <u>Ibid.</u>, p. 46.

Hedayat seems to be implying that if consciousness becomes powerful enough, then what it conceives becomes true. The breakdown occurs when the standard of reference is lost and one becomes a lucid, free-flowing consciousness through space and time. Without a tangible basis, the mind cannot discriminate and hence loses its capacity to judge. The end result is the surrender of consciousness to simple lucid awareness—a will-less state akin, but not equivalent to madness.

The narrator, though admittedly dissipated, is actually the most lucid and sane character in modern literature. But because his awareness transcends conventional modes of thought, the reader easily assumes him insane. On the contrary. The narrator is perceptive and perhaps even enlightened. A passage, as the narrator falls asleep, illustrates the clarity of his consciousness, the lucidity of his thought.

> As my eyes closed a dim, indistinct world began to take shape around me. It was a world of which I was the sole creator and which was in perfect harmony with my vision of reality. At all events it was far more real and natural to me than my waking world and presented no obstacle, no barrier, to my ideas. In it time and place lost their validity. My repressed lusts, my secret needs, which had begotten this dream, gave rise to shapes and to happenings which were beyond belief but which seemed natural to me. For a few moments after waking up I had no sense of time or place and doubted whether I really existed. It would seem that I myself created all my dreams and had long known the correct interpretation of them. [175]

With Hedayat's Weltanschauung it is no wonder that his own fate lay in committing suicide, for the horror of undifferentiated and yet lucid consciousness is too much for most men to bear. Hedayat further stacked the odds against himself with his pessimistic approach, for if life is "thought" to be a nightmare, then by virtue of idealistic premises it is necessarily so. On the other hand, if life is "thought" to be a meaningful dream then it must also be so. Such is the underlying theme of Hermann Hesse's intricate masterpiece The Glass Bead Game.

---

175. Ibid., pp. 86-87.

SECTION THREE

The Dream as Life

"Our truest life is when we are in dreams awake." [176]

—*Thoreau*

---

176. Henry David Thoreau, "A Week on the Concord and Merrimack Rivers" (1849) in <u>The Writings of Henry David Thoreau</u> (Boston: Houghton Mifflin, 1906), vol. 1, p. 316.

Meaningful Illusions
The Glass Bead Game of Life

In Hermann Hesse's last major novel, The Glass Bead Game, life is revealed as an infinitely complex dream—a dream paradoxically both real and unreal, an imaginary sequence of metaphysically interrelated ideas. The key to this enigmatic nature lies in "The Third Life" of Joseph Knecht which concludes the Nobel prize-winning story. By a literary circumlocution Hesse shows with subtlety the major theme of the novel—that life is a real dream which must be mastered, played upon, and ultimately dreamed to its fullest. Life, according to Hesse, is a game we must win.

On the surface, The Glass Bead Game is about an intellectual-mystical master—the Magister Ludi, Joseph Knecht. The novel traces the development of Joseph Knecht's life from childhood to member of Castalia (a scholarly monastic order) and eventually to the supreme position of Magister Ludi—master of the Glass Bead Game (a mental alchemy which interrelates all sciences and arts). However the real theme of The Glass Bead Game is actually hidden within the novel's own unique structure.

Hesse is playing his own Glass Bead Game by forcing the reader to analyze and follow the sophisticated development of the plot. And such a plot—the real plot—is not what it seems. The story of Joseph Knecht's rise and fall is not at issue here, for such a personal narrative is irrelevant to the real meaning of the book. (This is the reason Hesse entitled his masterpiece The Glass Bead Game rather than the more personal Americanized title of Magister Ludi.) What is at issue is the reality-illusion dichotomy central to the theme of Knecht's third life ("The Indian Life") and played upon symbolically throughout the remainder of the novel. The correlation of the two apparently dissociated segments results in the discovery of a unifying theme. The Glass Bead Game is itself the cosmic basis of life!—the flow of Maya ultimately mastered and made real. The novel hence becomes a game plan, a blueprint for the Glass Bead Game of life. The opening movement of the Game's novel beginning as follows.

"The Indian Life" is the imaginary alternative life envisioned by Joseph Knecht while still a student of Castalia. This youthful account is the story of one man's painful encounter with Maya—the illusory dream of life. Dasa, the hero of the story, is the archetypal prince who is cheated out of his rightful inheritance of the throne. Pursued by the rival false heir, Dasa takes refuge in the forest where he finds peace and security as the companion of an old ascetic hermit. Dasa eventually becomes intrigued by the spiritual recluse and asks to be taught about Maya. In brief, he dreams that he is reinstated as the rightful heir to the throne. He marries, has a child, loves and lives his life to the fullest only to realize in the end that it was only a dream— that life is itself only an unusually long dream. Dasa falls victim to the supreme "rude awakening," for as Hesse writes in the final pages of the novel:

> Suddenly the long years he had lived, the treasures cherished, the delights enjoyed, the pangs suffered, the fears endured, the despair he had tasted to the brink of death—all this had been taken from him, extinguished, reduced to nothingness. And yet not to nothingness! For the memory was there. The images had remained with him. . . .
>
> . . . All that crowded reality had been a dream. Perhaps, too, he had dreamed all that had happened previously . . . And was what he was experiencing this moment, what he saw before his eyes . . . together with what he was now thinking about it all—was not all this made of the same stuff? Was it not dream, illusion, Maya? And everything he would still experience in the future, would see with his eyes and feel with his hands, up to the moment of his death— was it any different in substance, any different in kind? It was all a game and a sham, all foam and dream. It was Maya, the whole lovely and frightful,

Evolutionary Consciousness

delicious and desperate kaleidoscope of life with its
searing delights, its searing griefs. [177]

Dasa thus becomes "disillusioned" with the world of "real" life.
Experiencing through a vivid dream the quintessential illusion of
life, he conversely realizes that life is in reality nothing more than a
dream, simply an illusion, though not a "simple" illusion, but rather
Maya, the paradoxical real illusion. And so Dasa abandons the realm
of human life as he learns the parable of the Ultimate Dream. Dasa
knows that for him life is no longer important and now dedicates his
energy towards the transcendent reality—the reality which takes place
beyond space and time, the spiritual realm of Castalia, The Glass Bead
Game of Life.

Dasa's story does not end here, nor does that of the novel itself,
for it must be remembered that "The Indian Life" is but a spiritual
vision from Joseph Knecht's youth, and Knecht does eventually grow
up to become the Magister Ludi—the Grand Metaphysician, the
alchemical manipulator of the mind. To be sequentially correct Hesse
should have placed the third life at the beginning of the story, but
this would obviously have destroyed the "Glass Bead Game" effect.
Instead, by placing the youthful writings at the end of the novel, Hesse
disorders the time frame, thus forcing the reader, if not literally then
at least figuratively, to return to the beginning and reexperience the
book. And such circular reflection results in two major realizations
which would otherwise have been lost.

The first realization is that the "game" and "dream," the
"Kaleidoscope of life" of Dasa's disillusionment is mastered by Joseph
Knecht as the Magister Ludi. The Glass Bead Game is in effect the
metaphysical interrelations underlying all life. It is an assimilation
and correlation of all knowledge, wisdom, creative arts, and sciences
since the beginning of time. It has, according to some, become
almost a religion. It is the supreme art work itself—the dynamic,
ever-changing, cosmic opera known as life. Knecht therefore masters
and refines the world of conceptual dreams which had so disillusioned
him while only a student of Castalia. He has conquered the "foam"
and "dream," the "Kaleidoscope" of Maya and become the supreme
Correlator of existence, the yoga master of life.

The second major realization arrived at by the juxtaposition of
"The Indian Life" with "The Life of Magister Ludi" is that Joseph

177. Hermann Hesse, The Glass Bead Game (New York: Holt, Rinehart and
Winston, Inc., 1969), pp. 555-556.

Knecht has not died in vain. Whereas the first theme of dream mastery comes from placing the third life before the main body of the novel, the second theme of Knecht's death comes from just the opposite sequence. By placing the youthful vision of "The Third Life" at the end of the novel, Hesse is concluding the story with an ingeniously paradoxical note of inspiration. "The Life of Magister Ludi" is one long and moving account of the rise and fall of an intellectual-mystical master. Knecht makes the supreme decision of his life concerning, not only his fate, but also the fate of Castalia. And yet on attempting to carry out his revolutionary plan by removing himself from the ivory-tower idealism of Castalia into the tangible world of "real" everyday life, Knecht dies in a freak accident on the first day of the rebellion. One may consider this ending ironic or tragic or pessimistic of Hesse, but one must not forget this is <u>not</u> the end of the book. "The Indian Life" concludes the sequence by informing the reader that the momentous life of Joseph Knecht rising to the Magister Ludi, this Castalian world of spiritual harmony breaking down into spiritual turmoil is, after all, only a dream, only Maya. And this death makes no difference in this world of illusions, for all that matters is to play the game, dream the dream, master the illusions to the fullest. Joseph Knecht dies . . . but the Glass Bead Game goes on. .. ..

Giorgio de Chirico. *The Purity of a Dream.* 1915

Creative Illusions

"Man is made by his belief. As he believes, so he is." [178]
—*Bhagavad-Gita*

According to Hesse, it is therefore the consciousness, the idealized processes, which are the meaning of life. Inner, creative awareness thus takes precedence over objective reality. Such is also the position of Hesse's predecessor, Friedrich Nietzsche.* However Nietzsche goes a step further than Hesse. According to his philosophy it is not only that subjective processes take precedence over objectivity, but that so-called "objectivity" does not even exist. Nietzsche denies the concept of an absolute, objective truth or frame of reference. Rather, what man is faced with is a multitude of varying and contradictory perspectives each of which is as valid or as invalid as the other. The only difference is in their subjective effects. All is error. And yet all is truth. Truth is perspectival. It is a relative opinion on the nature of existence. It varies. It is in flux.

Thus the only measure of value for truth is the degree to which it is useful or productive, the extent to which it can vitalize and enhance one's life. There is no other basis with which to make comparisons, for the concept of truth is meaningless. It is only a perspective. It may as well be called an illusion. And indeed Nietzsche himself considers these perspectives to be illusions. He distinguishes only between

---

* *Hesse was greatly influenced by Nietzsche, so much so that one of the characters in <u>The Glass Bead Game</u> is actually a thinly disguised version of Nietzsche himself.*

178. <u>Bhagavad-Gita</u>, Chapter 17, Stanza 3.

illusions that vitalize and those that devitalize, those that are healthy from those that are diseased, those that create from those that are stagnant or destroy. It is like a work of art which is only a subjective perspective. In a way it is a lie, it is biased and deceptive, and yet at the same time it is equally real, perhaps more real than one's life itself—because it is an ideal. It is one's own creation.

Nietzsche believes this should be the case with life. Life should be a work of art. For with both life and art it is all a matter of subjective experience and perspective. In fact Nietzsche claims that this is the only excuse for existence: "—for it is only as an aesthetic phenomenon that existence and the world are eternally justified--." [179]

Because it is only as something which can be molded into an ideal that such a chaotic substance can be defined. And it is only as a metaphysical artist—a dreamer of one's own dream—that life in any sense can become valid. George Bernard Shaw was deeply influenced by Nietzsche and fully agrees with this belief: "no person is real until he has been transmuted into a work of art." [180] Nietzsche and Shaw are thus advocating the creative conceptualization of life. Their philosophy is essentially that one should live and become one's dreams.

Such a philosophical approach has been demonstrated to parallel the nature of reality. For the universe is constantly changing. It is both relative and indeterminate. For this reason no structured approach is flexible enough to accommodate its scope. As physicist Fred Wolf maintains in his book Taking the Quantum Leap: "The order of the universe may be the order of our own minds." [181] Hence the only effective model for reality is that of the dynamic creative imagination. And such an imagination is best expressed through artistic idealizations or dreams.

Such a dream-reality approach however did not originate with Nietzsche and Shaw. It is present in Hinduism as the concept of "Maya": the dream-stuff of which all existence is composed. And indeed, even in primitive aboriginal tribes, the idea is present in varying forms. According to British anthropologist Francis Huxley:

The Aranda Aborigines call the original time—during

---

179. Friedrich Nietzsche, The Birth of Tragedy (and The Case of Wagner) (New York: Random House, Inc., 1967), p. 52.
180. Stephen Winsten, Days with Bernard Shaw (New York: Vanguard Press, Inc., 1949), p. 187.
181. Fred Wolf, Taking the Quantum Leap (San Francisco: Harper & Row, Publishers, Inc., 1981), p. 6.

which the world was fashioned—Alcheringa or 'the Dream-time' and other Aboriginal tribes use similar names. [182]

Thus it seems that the dream, one's creative unconscious and imagination is somehow perceived as being at the very basis of life, even among so-called "primitive" and "backward" cultures.

But what is all this superstitious talk of dreams? What is all this philosophical theorizing? Is it not all gibberish and mindless prattle? Is there any tangible evidence for believing imagination and thought to be real?

It would be a salve to one's belief system were this all conjecture, but the challenge is both serious and concrete. There is definite experimental evidence that subjective mental processes can affect external reality, and not merely one's perception of it. There is objectively demonstrable and repeatable proof for the ability of the mind to mold "reality" to one's thoughts. The agency is not yet understood, for it seems contrary to all rational concepts of science, and thus for centuries it has been relegated to the mere level of an unexplained curio. However the agency has very practical and beneficial applications. It is objectively verifiable. It provides "hard results." And thus it has persisted and manifested itself in whatever guise possible: witchcraft, sorcery, occult magic, entertainment, and (more recently) generalized medical treatment. However it wasn't until 1958 that it achieved official recognition. Despite denouncements as quackery, its viability led to its acceptance by the American Medical Association as a valid form of medical treatment. That treatment or agency, so long denied credibility, is the power to alter mental frameworks through subconscious processes—in other words, the mysterious power of hypnosis.

Hypnosis is a modern-day enigma. Psychologists are puzzled over just how and why it works. Theories are advanced, and then criticisms and modifications ad infinitum, and yet no one is really any closer to the truth (much less even to a consensus agreement). For the process is simply not understood—yet it works!

What seems to be involved is a temporary suspension of normal belief patterns. These reality frameworks or programs are somehow capable of being modified or replaced by new programming sets— sets that are often far removed from what was originally believed or what is actually present in the external world. Thus, when activated,

---

182. Francis Huxley, op. cit., p. 120.

these mental sets often produce bizarre results—and not just in one's subjective perception of reality, but within physical reality itself.

Experimental studies by Stanford psychiatrist, David Spiegel, show that successful hypnotic suggestions are not simply delusions or attempts to fool or please the hypnotist. Rather, they physically alter energy consumption and neural pathways in the brain. The brain is reset to an alternate sensory program.

The experiment has variants, but all involve either black and white or colored rectangles shown to a subject who has been placed under hypnosis. The subject is placed in a PET (positron emission tomography) scanner which shows the energy uptake in the brain's fusiform gyrus which becomes active when perceiving color.

While viewing colored rectangles, the subject is told that they are becoming gray. The fusiform gyrus responds by dramatically decreasing activity. Conversely, viewing black and white rectangles and told that they are colored makes the fusiform gyrus light up. Strangely, when just told to imagine color, only the right hemisphere fusiform gyrus lights up.

> Under hypnosis, though, both sides of the brain became active— just as in regular sight. Under hypnosis, imagination seemed to take on the quality of a hallucination. . . . "The realms of imagination and perception are not entirely distinct," Spiegel says. [183]

In other words, by simply thinking you don't see color, the brain physically shuts down the perception of color. How much of reality is shut down through cultural pressure or personal bias making it physically impossible to perceive what we have been told (or tell ourselves) not to believe? Spiegel concludes:

> We tend to think that the brain processes raw information and we make sense of it afterwards. But it turns out, especially in studies of hypnosis, that we can re-set the brain, that we can change the way the brain actually perceives information. So it's not that it reacts differently to the same input. It changes what the input is." [184]

183. Michael Abrams, "Hypnosis Works" in Discover (Waukesha, Wisconsin: Kalmbach Publishing Company, November, 2004).
184. "Can Our Minds Be Hacked?" in Through the Wormhole with Morgan Freeman: Season Four (Discovery Communications, LLC for the Science Channel, produced by Revelations Entertainment LLC for Science, 2014).

Perhaps the most remarkable and practical aspect of hypnosis is its ability to produce local analgesia (or insensitivity to pain). Simply as a result of mental suggestion or voluntary delusion (either self-induced or with the assistance of a hypnotist) one can circumvent or ignore the physical sensation of pain. Teeth can be extracted without anesthetics, and yet the fully-conscious patient will show no discomfort or distress. Pins and needles can be driven deep into the arm, and yet the calm victim will not object, for to him the sensation is at most a mere tickle. In fact, C. Scott Moss explains in his book Hypnosis in Perspective that:

> A hundred years ago J. Esdaile, working in India, performed over 3,000 well-documented operations, many of them involving major amputations. Yet the mechanism involved remains so little understood (it is so incredible that "just talk" could effect such startling results) that today when an operation or childbirth is performed using hypnosis it still receives sensational publicity.[185]

On the other hand (as opposed to inducing analgesia) a subject may show violent reactions to the mere touch of a feather, believing the suggestion that he has been stabbed by a knife. Somehow physiological processes are not only being circumvented, but also altered merely as a result of subjective thoughts. Belief systems are thus somehow capable of changing the physical processes of the body. And it is not simply a matter of a distortion in perception, for actual physical changes or damages will occur according to the corresponding suggestion. The belief that a feather is actually a burning, iron rod can cause welts to form on some subject's skin. And the belief that no bleeding will occur can result in only slight or superficial bleeding while extracting teeth.

It thus appears that the mind, the power of belief, is strong enough to mediate physical changes in objective reality. Further physical effects of hypnosis include partial or total catalepsy; paralysis of

---

185. C. Scott Moss, Hypnosis in Perspective (New York: The Macmillan Company, 1965), p. 53.

major muscle groups; blindness or loss of hearing; control of capillary bleeding, saliva flow, vomiting, gagging, and other involuntary physiological processes or responses.

Furthermore, many of these powers and effects of hypnosis are paralleled by other consciousness-altering practices. Meditation, biofeedback, acupuncture, and trance show similar effects upon what was previously considered involuntary, "autonomic," bodily processes. Indeed, even among the mentally disturbed, supernormal subconscious control over physiological mechanisms are evident. "Glove anaesthesia," paralysis, and psychosomatic blindness or deafness are symptomatic of certain forms of hysteria. Cataleptic postures, hallucinations, and bizarre thought patterns are indicative of psychoses such as schizophrenia. Thus it appears that the power of the mind, the power of thought or belief, is not confined to the manifestations of hypnosis. Rather it is present along with nearly any serious, concentrated, and absorbing activity of the mind.

However the argument may be made that these are, after all, merely changes in the subject himself. It can be rationalized that these altered states simply demonstrate the existence of previously unknown processes or links between the mind and body—latent abilities which do not necessarily contradict the physical laws of science. Such an argument may be valid to some degree, but it must be remembered that the laws of physics are themselves being revised. The new framework shows an interconnecting causal network between the observer and the observed, a relative universe which is indeterminate and in flux. As such, the boundaries between subjective and objective are no longer clearly defined. Just where does one distinguish between the mind as subject and the body as object? Just where can one say that thoughts have been made real? When one can fly through the air? When physical laws are defied?

Numerous incidents have been documented of a strange, esoteric practice which apparently defies the laws of physical reality. The practice is not associated with the controversial field of psychic phenomena simply because its existence is too well-documented. The phenomenon is known to occur. The controversy is merely over how and why it happens. The practice is briefly described as follows. After a period of weeks or months of preparation, a group of "initiates" (both men and women) come filing out of a temple led by their native village priest. In something akin to an ecstatic trance they walk, one after another, over a bed of hot coals. Most escape the ordeal without a mark. Many actually seem to enjoy the experience: dancing about, grinding their feet into the burning embers. A small percentage (the failures) suffer severe burns and must be hospitalized. A few have actually been burned to death. The phenomenon is real. It has been filmed and verified by reputable eye-witness reports. Accounts of it have appeared in <u>National Geographic Magazine</u>. It has been witnessed by scientists, journalists, scholars, diplomats, and tourists. The question is thus not whether or not the phenomenon of "fire-walking" actually occurs, but rather why it occurs—why physical laws are seemingly defied—why most initiates succeed and yet some fail.

The natives and the priests claim that it is all a matter of faith. Belief alone determines whether or not God is with them and will protect them from harm. And yet, objectively speaking, every one of them should suffer harm, because it should be physically impossible to walk barefoot over hot coals and escape unscathed. In one such fire-walk a member of a "National Geographic" team measured the heat from the pit of coals with an optical pyrometer. The pyrometer registered 1,328 degrees Fahrenheit. Wads of paper thrown into the bed of coals, according to another report of a fire-walk, were seen to burst into flames before touching the ground. The phenomenon does not appear to involve trickery. Laboratory studies of fire-walkers carried out by Indian scientists substantiate the claim: fire-walking is real. For some reason, certain people can walk upon and even grind their feet into coals over 1,000 degrees Fahrenheit without being burned. And by all known physical laws this is impossible. In <u>The Crack in the Cosmic Egg</u> Joseph Chilton Pearce describes the only "Western" experiment on fire-walking undertaken at the time.

> It would seem that fire-walking could never prove amenable to laboratory testing, but at Surrey, England, in 1935-36, the English Society for Psychical Research ran a series of tests on two Indian fakirs imported expressly for the purpose. The tests were graded by physicians, chemists, physicists, and psychologists of Oxford. The Indians walked the fire under control conditions, under the skeptical and probing eyes of science itself. . . . No chemicals were used, no preparations made, they repeated the performances under a variety of conditions and over a period of several weeks, on demand. Surface temperatures were between 450-500° Centigrade, the

interior temperatures 1400° C. There was no trickery or hallucination. [186]

Thus it appears that the mind, one's subjective thoughts, can alter not only one's perception of reality, but also physical reality itself. The obvious question is why such powers are not more widely known?—why mores scientists do not investigate such phenomena?—why the only Western experiment on fire-walking (prior to the publication of Pearce's book) had to be carried out by The Society for Psychical Research in 1936?

The answer is that modern science is resisting a paradigm shift—because to admit that such phenomena exist is to admit that our view of reality is wrong, that the dream, the "mumbo jumbo," the creative unconscious is real. And perhaps far more real than would be comfortable to believe. And thus we ignore such threatening assaults upon conventional modes of reality, "pigeonholing" ourselves in a mental prison from which we do not wish to escape.

C. Scott Moss describes the resistance to such new paradigms in relation to hypnosis:

> Psychologists have been dissuaded from active inquiry by the very real "career risk" occasioned by the suspicious attitudes of skeptical colleagues. . . . As a consequence, opportunities for formal instruction concerning hypnosis are decidedly restricted. Few graduate departments of psychology include the subject in their curriculum, and the typical course in abnormal psychology tends to represent hypnosis largely as an historical curiosity. Even medical schools provide little formal training in the treatment potentialities implicit in this technique. While an enormous amount of research is needed in order to achieve a more adequate understanding of hypnosis, few psychology faculty members have ventured into the area, and the prudent graduate student is well advised to avoid the complications inherent in a thesis or dissertation on the topic. [187]

---

186. Joseph Chilton Pearce, The Crack in the Cosmic Egg (New York: Pocket Books, 1971), pp. 110-111.
187. Moss, op. cit., pp. VII-VIII.

Thus, even in such a substantiated field as hypnosis the prejudice is strong against those involved. The validity of the phenomenon is recognized, but little else. And so it appears that belief in mind over matter is being resisted in order to preserve our cherished consensus reality. The evolution of consciousness is being denied in the name of comfort and security. But perhaps the reason for this resistance lies merely in the inability to conceptually rationalize the phenomenon. Through what physical mechanisms does this subjective-objective interaction take place? Just how is it possible for the dream to be real?

According to Italian physicist Jack Sarfatti, gravity may be the medium through which these subjective-objective interactions flow. In his view, thought can structure reality through bio-gravitational fields which contain mini-black holes or quantum singularities. Through mental projection these fields can be warped or altered, resulting in transcendental modes through which objective reality can change. There is thus a "quantum-interconnectedness" in the universe among which imagination and thought can leap. This may sound like New-Age hocus-pocus. However, string/ M theory recently proposed that gravity might be a mode of communication between the eleven dimensions of space-time. Gravity may be what binds the eleven dimensions together, and that is the reason it appears so weak in our universe.

While Sarfatti may have been one of the most radical of the "new physicists," other more conventional explanations for quantum mechanics are still essentially the same. Astrophysicist John Wheeler explains the paradoxes of the new physics (particularly the "Einstein-Podolsky-Rosen effect") in terms of what he calls a "participatory universe."

> Useful as it is under everyday circumstances to say that the world exists "out there" independent of us, that view can no longer be upheld. There is a strange sense in which this is a "participatory universe." [188]

However, in a paper which he submitted to a symposium of the American Association for the Advancement of Science, Wheeler argues against the wild claims of "occult" physicists like Sarfatti.

---

188. John A. Wheeler quoted by Bruce Rosenblum and Fred Kuttner, Quantum Enigma: Physics Encounters Consciousness (New York: Oxford University Press, Inc., 2011), p. 219.

Instead, what Wheeler proposes is that the observer is merely part of an interacting system with physical reality. The observer participates not only in the perception, but also in the determination of the reality to be perceived. Thus there is a dynamic interplay, a "participatory universe"—which nevertheless has no need for recourse to any occult or paranormal laws. Wheeler concludes his paper with the declamatory statement:

> ...let us continue to insist on the centuries-long tradition of science, in which we exclude all mysticism and insist on the rule of reason. And let no one use the Einstein-Podolsky-Rosen experiment to claim that information can be transmitted faster than light, or to postulate any so-called "quantum interconnectedness" between separate consciousness. Both are baseless. Both are mysticism. Both are moonshine. [189]

Wheeler's argument is analogous to the argument against hypnotic powers being evidence of the mind's influence over physical reality. Just as some would maintain that such effects are merely the result of previously unknown psychophysical interactions within the subject himself—so too, Wheeler is claiming that no paranormal explanations are necessary with quantum mechanics, but rather simply a reconsideration of the observer as an integral part and co-determiner of the universe. Hence no mystical "quantum interconnectedness" need be invoked. Being necessarily enmeshed in physical reality, the observer merely interacts with and thus influences the reality of which he is part.

And yet, strange as it may seem, both Wheeler and Sarfatti (although employing different approaches and perspectives) wind up with the same conclusion: the observer, through his own subjective framework and thoughts, can influence and determine the actual nature of the reality that he sees. In both views one's conceptions have been "manifested" in the external world. Physicist Henry P. Stapp of the Lawrence Berkeley Laboratory explains that quantum mechanics has a "perfectly natural place for consciousness, a place

---

189. John A. Wheeler, "Not Consciousness but the Distinction Between the Probe and the Probed as Central to the Elemental Quantum Act of Observation" (in The Role of Consciousness in the Physical World, edited by Robert G. Jahn), (Boulder, Colorado: Westview Press, Inc., 1981), p. 98.

that allows each conscious event, conditioned, but not bound, by any known law of nature, to grasp a possible large-scale metastable pattern of neuronal activity in the brain, and convert its status from 'possible' to 'actual.'"[190]

> The most important consequence of this altered vision of nature is the place it provides for human minds. Consciousness is no longer forced to be an impotent spectator to a mechanically determined flow of physical events.[191]

According to physicists Rosenblum and Kuttner:

> Quantum theory thus denies the existence of a physically real world independent of its observation.[192]

> It tells us that physical reality is created by observation, and it has "spooky actions" instantaneously influencing events far from each other—without any physical force involved. Seen from a human perspective, quantum mechanics has physics encountering consciousness.[193]

They go on to extend quantum observation principles from the micro-world to the macro-world:

> A photon, an electron, an atom, a molecule, in principle any object, can be either compact or widely spread out. You can show an object to be either bigger than a loaf of bread or smaller than an atom. You can choose which of these two contradictory features to demonstrate. The physical reality of an object depends on how you choose to look at it.[194]

Perhaps the best closing commentary on this debate comes from

190. Henry P. Stapp, <u>Mind, Matter, and Quantum Mechanics</u> (New York: Springer-Verlag, 1993), p. 38.
191. <u>Ibid.</u>, p. 213.
192. Rosenblum and Kuttner, <u>op. cit.</u>, p. 7.
193. Rosenblum and Kuttner, <u>op. cit.</u>, p. XI
194. Rosenblum and Kuttner, <u>op. cit.</u>, p. 72.

the Nobel prize-winning physicist Eugene Wigner. According to Wigner, consciousness plays an important role in quantum mechanics, much more so than scientists like Wheeler would like to believe. In fact, belief is really the key issue here. Rather than simply interacting and determining as a consequence of interactions and relative perceptual frameworks, Wigner (like Sarfatti and Stapp) favors a more active element to thought. To him it is more the belief, not merely the interacting physical mechanism, which determines reality. And thus Wigner, Sarfatti, and Stapp see a more "mystical," consciously-oriented basis underlying the universe. Or as Wigner states in his book <u>Symmetries and Reflections</u>:

> The physico-chemical conditions and properties of the substrate not only create the consciousness, they also influence its sensations most profoundly. Does, conversely, the consciousness influence the physico-chemical conditions? In other words, does the human body deviate from the laws of physics, as gleaned from the study of inanimate nature? The traditional answer to this question is, "No": the body influences the mind but the mind does not influence the body. [195]

> The recognition that physical objects and spiritual values have a very similar kind of reality has contributed in some measure to my mental peace. . . . At any rate, it is the only known point of view which is consistent with quantum mechanics. [196]

> ...the very study of the external world led to the conclusion that the content of the consciousness is an ultimate reality. [197]

Wigner's mentor, John von Neumann, laid the mathematical foundation for quantum mechanics. He himself

> merely hinted at consciousness-created reality in dark parables. His followers, notably, London, Bauer,

---

195. Eugene Wigner, <u>Symmetries and Reflections</u> (Bloomington, Indiana: Indiana University Press, 1967), p. 178.
196. <u>Ibid.</u>, p. 192.
197. <u>Ibid.</u>, p. 172.

and Wigner, boldly carried von Neumann's argument to its logical conclusion: If we wholeheartedly accept von Neumann's picture of quantum theory, they say, a consciousness-created reality is the inevitable outcome. [198]

Physicist Evan Walker sums up the theories and experimental findings of quantum mechanics. The paradoxes are undeniable and a paradigm shift is needed. In his book, <u>The Physics of Consciousness</u>, he boldly proclaims:

> We must recognize that objective reality is a flawed concept . . . Our entire conception of reality must now be rethought. We stand at the threshold of a revolution in thinking that transcends anything that has happened in a thousand years. Now the observer, consciousness, something self-like or mind-like, becomes a provable part of a richer reality than physics or any science has ever dared to envision...
>
> This revised view of reality in which we see the observer and the consciousness as central to reality itself is as significant as if we had found the key to the soul. Perhaps that is what has been found here. [199]

---

198. Nick Herbert, <u>Elemental Mind: Human Consciousness and the New Physics</u> (New York: Penguin Books USA Inc., 1993), p. 249.
199. Walker, <u>op. cit.</u>, pp. 137-8.

Evolutionary Consciousness

"What we need is imagination. We have to find a new view of the world." [200]
—*Richard P. Feynman*

"Imagination is more important than knowledge." [201]
—*Albert Einstein*

Reality is a dream, a dynamic, ever-changing artwork synthesized by the mind. We create our lives, our holograms, by projecting our thoughts and will into our mode of perception. And these modes or frameworks are in turn capable of infinite mutability through imagination. We can thus dream our own dreams rather than accept the dreams or nightmares of others. This power to alter one's conceptions, to imagine one's reality, is latent within all human beings. It is simply a matter of belief, an expression of one's dreams. And thus, only those who literally have the strength of their convictions, the strength to dream, remain at the forefront of evolutionary consciousness.

The objection can be made that this is all well and good for the elite, for those who can walk over fires or jab needles into their arms, but what about the average person?—the 95 percent of the population who are not "deep trance" hypnotic subjects or who cannot dedicate their lives to yogic meditation? The answer is that it doesn't matter. No special discipline is necessary in order to effect a change, for it is

200. Richard P. Feynman, The Character of Physical Law (Cambridge, Massachusetts: Massachussetts Institute of Technology Press, 1965), p. 171.
201. Albert Einstein, as quoted in "What Life Means to Einstein: An Interview by George Sylvester Viereck" in The Saturday Evening Post, 202 (26 October 1929), p. 117.

all in the mind, a matter of attitude and belief: the faith that can move mountains, the dreams that we all dream every single night.

Perhaps the most impressive demonstration of this inherent ability comes from experiments on visual direction constancy. When a neuro-muscular blocking agent paralyzes the muscles of a subject's eyes a curious phenomenon occurs. The mere intention of eye movement creates the visual illusion of movement. An actual shift is seen in the visual field. And yet the eyes have remained immobile! No change has actually taken place because the muscles of the eyes are no longer functional. And yet a visual shift nevertheless appears in the direction of the intended movement. Robert Welch summarizes the implications of various studies:

> ...the <u>attempt</u> to move the eyes leads to the experience of illusory visual motion or to a jump in apparent visual direction...Thus, it is the intent, not the actual eye movements (and concomitant neural inflow), that determines the perceptual outcome. [202]

Psychologist R.L. Gregory remarks further on this strange phenomenon:

> The eye/head system, then, does not work by actual movement of the eyes, but by commands to move them. It works even when the eyes do not obey the commands. It is surprising that command signals can give rise to perception of movement: we usually think of movement perception as always coming from the eyes, not from a source deep in the brain controlling them. [203]

And hence, subjective processes can overcome physical limitations. By simply idealizing our world the shapes of reality will begin to change. What is amazing about this experiment is that it shows just how generalized or inherent this ability actually is, for anyone can experience the phenomenon were he to paralyze his eyes. What it signifies is the active role the observer plays in

202. Robert B. Welch, <u>Perceptual Modification: Adapting to Altered Sensory Environments</u> (New York: Academic Press, Inc., 1978), p. 163.
203. R.L. Gregory, <u>Eye and Brain</u> (New York: McGraw-Hill Book Company, 1977), pp. 100-101.

the way the world is perceived. Rather than passively interpreting incoming sensations, we can actually create them. As shown in the random-dot stereograms, we idealize reality before it is seen. The double-slit experiment shows clearly that the way we "choose" to view the universe consequently determines the outcome that is desired. Reality is an interpretation. It can change through the perspective or consciousness of the observer.

The premise of this book may seem fantastic. But forty years ago, Sarfatti's proposal that mini-black holes and gravitational forces are the glue through which quantum-interconnectedness is maintained, also seemed fanciful, New-Age mysticism. And yet now, cutting-edge physics is lending credence to these claims. String/M theory has proposed that gravity is what connects the theoretical eleven dimensions of reality, and therefore is a possible means of inter-dimensional communication. String/M theory allows for time travel, faster-than-light particles, alternate realities, and parallel universes. Physicist Fred Alan Wolf suggests that lucid dreaming may itself be a doorway to these parallel universes. "Like Pribram, Wolf believes our minds create the illusion of reality 'out there' through the same kind of processes studied by Bekesy."[204] In this sophisticated theoretical framework could not an objective-idealist universe be true?

Physicist Amit Goswami defends this theoretical interpretation of reality. In his book, The Self-Aware Universe, Goswami posits monistic idealism (a variant under the epistemological category of objective idealism) as the underlying principle of the universe. Fred Alan Wolf maintains in support of Goswami:

> There is too much quantum weirdness around, too many experiments showing that the objective world... is an illusion of our thinking.

Wolf further explains Goswami's position that we must:

> ...give up that precious assumption that there is an objective reality "out there" independent of consciousness. It says even more, that the universe

---

204. Michael Talbot, The Holographic Universe (New York: Harper Collins Publishers, 1991), p. 66.

is "self-aware" and that it is consciousness itself that creates the physical world. [205]

According to Goswami himself:

> . . . both idealism and realism can be valid. Both are right. For if the brain-mind itself is an object in a nonlocal consciousness that encompasses all reality, then what we call objective empirical reality is within this consciousness. It is a theoretical idea of this consciousness—thus idealism is valid. [206]

> I trust my intuition that the idealist interpretation of quantum mechanics is the correct one. Of all the interpretations, this is the only one that promises to take physics into a new arena: the arena of the brain-mind-consciousness problem. [207]

Further corroboration comes from none other than Doctor Robert P. Lanza (Time Magazine's "The 100 Most Influential People"—April 2014). While most notable for his work on stem-cell research and cloning, Lanza nevertheless delves headlong into quantum mechanics and epistemology. In his book, Biocentrism, he argues that the mind creates reality through mere perception or quantum observation and interaction. "Reality is not 'there' with definite properties waiting to be discovered but actually comes into being depending upon the actions of the observer." [208] This is an objective-idealist principle: reality is influenced, shaped, and molded by the way we perceive. In his appearance in "Through the Wormhole" he explains how different observers see the universe in different ways. Perception and awareness is relative and subjective. And because the world is influenced by the observer, reality and the universe aren't static and external.

> It's not an object. It's an active process that actually involves our consciousness...Reality begins and ends

---

205. Amit Goswami, The Self-Aware Universe (New York: Penguin Putnam, Inc., 1993), p. XV.
206. Ibid., p. 144.
207. Ibid., p. 145.
208. Robert Lanza with Bob Berman, Biocentrism: How Life and Consciousness are the Keys to Understanding the True Nature of the Universe (Dallas: BenBella Books, Inc., 2009), p. 101.

with the observer. [209]

Although seemingly outlandish, there may be more to the universe than what common-sense, ordinary reality would have us believe. In the late nineteenth century, scientists confidently proclaimed that all major discoveries had been made. Before the Wright brothers, the esteemed <u>Scientific American</u> published papers proving the impossibility of manned air flight. The theory of continental drift was originally deemed laughable by the scientific community. In the 1930's Swiss astronomer Fritz Zwicky reasoned that not enough visible matter was holding galaxies together in groups. He proposed the term "dark matter" for this missing mass and its consequent gravitational effect. His views were considered "science fiction." Now the existence of dark matter has been proven by the gravitational lensing of distant galaxies as well as by Vera Rubin's mass distribution study of spiral galaxies. And in 2011 astronomers Perlmutter, Schmidt, and Riess were awarded the Nobel Prize for discovering the accelerating expansion of the universe, thus providing evidence for the existence of "dark energy." Dark matter and dark energy are now considered the major component of the universe, binding together its form and structure. This "science-fiction fantasy" is now our fantastic reality.

Einstein himself failed to accept the idea of an expanding universe, which his own equations allowed for as a real possibility. Instead, he championed a static, steady-state universe and then fudged his math by incorporating a "cosmological constant" to keep the universe stable—a lack of foresight which others have claimed was "the greatest blunder" of his life. Furthermore, this greatest blunder (if extrapolated upon and refined) could have been the precursor for dark energy and dark matter. Much to his regret, Einstein also originally rejected the possibility of black holes which are now a known fact to both astrophysicists and the lay public. If a visionary genius such as Einstein was guilty of shortsightedness, then how much more so is the average man on the street? Each generation believes they are at the pinnacle of understanding and wisdom. Will this hubris keep us closed-minded about the future as well?

And even if tangible evidence and theoretical support were lacking, it wouldn't really make a difference. For the very premise of this book is that it is only a matter of unerring belief. The dream, the

---

209. "Is the Universe Alive?" from "Through The Wormhole With Morgan Freeman: Season Three" (Produced by Revelations Entertainment and The Incubator for Science, 2012 Discovery Communications LLC, Laura Verklan—director).

inner self, takes precedence over the external. Could it be the dream that has control? Could it be the ultimate arbiter of reality?

In his most memorable speech, President Kennedy paraphrased the Serpent in George Bernard Shaw's <u>Back to Methuselah.</u> He summarized the philosophy of <u>Evolutionary Consciousness</u> most eloquently: "Some men see things as they are and say, 'Why?' I dream things that never were and I say, 'Why not?'" Humanity has been catapulted into the future by those with visions and the strength to dream.

In closing, repeating physicist Brian Greene's view of Susskind and Gerard't Hooft's String/membrane universe:

> The laws of physics would act as the universe's laser, illuminating the real processes of the cosmos— processes taking place on a thin, distant surface—and generating the holographic illusions of daily life. [210]

And paradoxically, as <u>The Endless Dream</u> ends:

> Half asleep, dazed by the illusion of life, his soul wandered back and lingered in the bright, crystal cavern of his dream. [211]

These illusions can be molded to fit one's own dream. Or as Novalis states so succinctly:

> Life must not be a novel that is given to us,
>
> but one that is made by us. [212]

---

210. Brian Greene, <u>op. cit.</u>, pp. 482-3.
211. Anonymous, <u>The Endless Dream, op. cit.</u>.
212. Novalis, from "Logological Fragments" in <u>Novalis: Philosophical Writings</u> (Albany: State University of New York Press, 1997), p. 66.

EXEMPLI GRATIA

"In the beginning was the word..and the word was God." [213]

—*John I:I*

"We are what we think. All that we are arises with our thoughts. With our thoughts, we make the world." [214]

—*Buddha*

---

213. The Holy Bible (King James Version) St. John 1:1.
214. Buddha, The Dhammapada: The sayings of the Buddha, Thomas Byrom (translator)(Boston: Shambhala Publications, Inc., 1993), p. 1.

A True Life - Story

"Wayne was sitting at the table sipping

his coffee, trying to compose himself...
                                his mind...
                                his thoughts..."

Here I was sitting in a cafe sipping coffee, trying to write a story.
But the words wouldn't come—I couldn't think of what to say—and
so I was just gazing off in a daze. I don't know how long it had been,
for the fog seemed timeless, but suddenly I heard voices from the
booth behind me. Strangely, they seemed to be talking about me, not
about myself personally, but about my whole life, my situation, the
very reason that brought me here, that sat me down in this booth to
write. And what's even stranger, the voices seemed familiar.

"So what are you saying?" said a young woman's voice. "What
do you mean, life is a dream?" Her voice had an English accent, a
skeptical haughty tone. "You mean that none of this is real?—that if I
hit you with this ashtray it's not going to hurt?"

I looked down and saw that my previously impotent pen was now
scribbling away, trying to capture every moment of the conversation.
And yet I was already lagging behind. Thank God for the pause. My
heart was only now catching up with the beat. My pen was only now
feeling the rhythm of what was said.

"You don't understand," said a young man's voice. "When I say life
is a dream I don't mean that nothing is real. I mean that everything
is real. It's just that we have the power to imagine and create. And
that imagination and creativity can shape reality—just as it shapes
a dream." He was excited and enthusiastic, ready to overflow with
energy. It was the nervous impulsiveness that one hears in lunatics,

religious fanatics, and good story-tellers. He was totally immersed in and convinced of everything he said. "It's like a story or movie. In fact it's just like the movie 'The French Lieutenant's Woman.' You saw it?"

"Yes, I really liked it, but I don't see what you mean. How do you get 'life is a dream' from that?"

"It's the whole point of the movie. You have an actor and an actress who play the part of romantic lovers in Victorian England. In real life the two also become lovers. Their lives and their roles somewhat entangle and parallel. But at the end of their Victorian roles the two lovers are brought together. Whereas at the end of shooting the movie the modern-day romantic counterpart abruptly stops. At the end of the movie the actor tries to catch the actress before she leaves the set. He rushes to the window as the actress is taking off in a sports car. He calls out—and I don't know whether this was even conscious on his part—but he calls out not her real name, but rather the name of the person she was playing."

"Yes, I got all that, but what has that to do with dreams?"

"It's that fiction or dreams are more powerful and meaningful than real life. In the imaginary Victorian setting the two lovers find true love. It's like a fairy tale. But in real life it's all messed up. Nothing comes out right. The actor has fallen in love with the actress, paralleling the script of the movie. She also feels for him, and both see the possible idealization—the potential reenactment of the movie, the making of the dream come true, but she becomes 'practical' and chooses 'reality' instead."

"But that's the way life is!" said the English woman sounding somewhat annoyed. "Things don't always work out the way we want them or the way they should. It's not all a fairy tale. Meaningless and absurd things happen all the time."

"But they don't have to. That's the point. If we all lived our lives like a meaningful story then everything would be meaningful. I once knew a guy who never let anything get him down. He looked at life as a movie with himself as the star. Any accidents or absurdities were simply part of the plot. They were meaningful intrusions, gambles and challenges. If he got fired it meant that it was time for him to change scenes. If he lost his love then it simply meant that he was supposed to find another. If he was late then he simply wasn't supposed to be there on time, something else had been prepared and was awaiting him along the way. He was constantly projecting these interpretations onto life. And not surprisingly this positive attitude molded reality to his tastes. He was always ready and actively engaged when the 'moment' came."

A pause allowed me to catch up with the thoughts and turn to the next page.

"You see, if we all believed in the dream, then life would be a dream. And in fact it's because life is a dream that it has become a nightmare. There are many who perversely insist on having a nightmare, and who are intent on including everyone else in their nightmare. Thank God there are at least some who still believe in the dream. Like that actor in the movie. I think the most moving, most beautiful part was at the very end. After she speeds off in the sports car, he flops down on the floor of the dark and empty room. People are partying both inside and outside the house. He is dejected, his hopes and dreams have died. And then suddenly there is the image of Victorian England. A scene on the river. The two lovers in a small boat on a bright sunny day—rowing leisurely away to find their dream. And with that my own tears began to flow. Because you see, it meant that the dream still exists. The dream is the ideal. It's what's meaningful and lasting."

"I took it to mean that it was just what he was imagining. How it might have been had things been different."

"I don't think so," said the man's voice as though he had thought it out beforehand. "Because if that were so, then he should have imagined them together in a modern-day setting. But he didn't. He imagined the Victorian, the idealized setting. Another thing is that each Victorian scene was previously shown to be the result of an actual filming. Each time they showed a scene, it had been acted out and filmed. It was part of the script. But the movie set had been dismantled. The filming was over. And yet we have the last scene, the movie continues, the dream is real."

I imagined her nodding reluctantly in agreement, and so I wrote it down.

"And the last point," he continued, "is that this was the closing scene to 'The French Lieutenant's Woman.' The movie, the credits, it all ends and fades out with the two lovers rowing off into the distance. Once again emphasizing the primacy of the dream over real life. The fairy-tale beauty was the closing commentary on this movie of life. And what more appropriate ending: an ideal work of art saying that only idealizations are real."

"All right," said the English voice, finally relenting, but still defiant. "I can see how it all fits. And I can see how novels and movies and dreams are more meaningful and beautiful than real life. But by God, how can you make real life any different?"

"By simply living your life as though it were a meaningful story. Acting out each moment as though it were your part."

"But that's absurd. You can't go through life thinking everything you say and do is meaningful, because it isn't."

"But that's only because you think it isn't. If you thought it was, then it would be. That's where the dream-element enters. Things are, or can become, exactly what you make them."

"I still don't buy it. You mean if I brush my teeth meaningfully, then the whole act will become meaningful?"

"Yes, that's it. Or maybe you'll just become aware of the meaning inherent in the act. It's the same with Zen Buddhism. The simplest task, the raking of leaves, becomes filled with significance. Every daily chore is imbued with a meaningful essence of its own. If you look at things this way, if you live your life this way, then suddenly everything becomes more real. It's like suddenly you're in a movie or novel in which everything exists for some reason or purpose. Sartre's half-open door.* No more accidents or absurdities. For we can create or enact the scene or story as we please. We become the writer, the director, and the actor of our lives. We become responsible for our existence. We become responsible for life. It's just like what Nietzsche said: 'Life is justified only as a work of art.' Because works of art can be playfully experimented with, they can be molded into an ideal."

A rustling from their booth meant they were about to leave. But I still hadn't finished! Down the hallway, someone opened the front door half-way! They were still talking as they stood and gathered their belongings. I wanted to glance backward to see their faces, to see them as they really were (not as I had imagined them), but more important was to get down everything exactly as it was said.

"You see, it is fiction and imagination, it is the dream and the ideal that can contain perfection. For the flaws are eliminated. Everything flows according to plan. It's what Hermann Hesse said in his novel, <u>Demian</u>: how works of art are more real than the artists themselves. And how next to them we ourselves are nothing..."

They were leaving. And yet I was still writing it down. I was scribbling frantically, trying to finish so that I could catch a glimpse, trying to capture the words before they were lost forever in the void.

" ...works of art are more real...than the artists themselves... And how next to them... we ourselves... are nothing..."

I turned around and looked. But there was no one there. I turned back to the pages of my story. A feverish chill passed through me as I put down my pen

---

* *Sartre explains that a half-open door in a story or novel must have some meaning. Otherwise, it would never have been mentioned.*

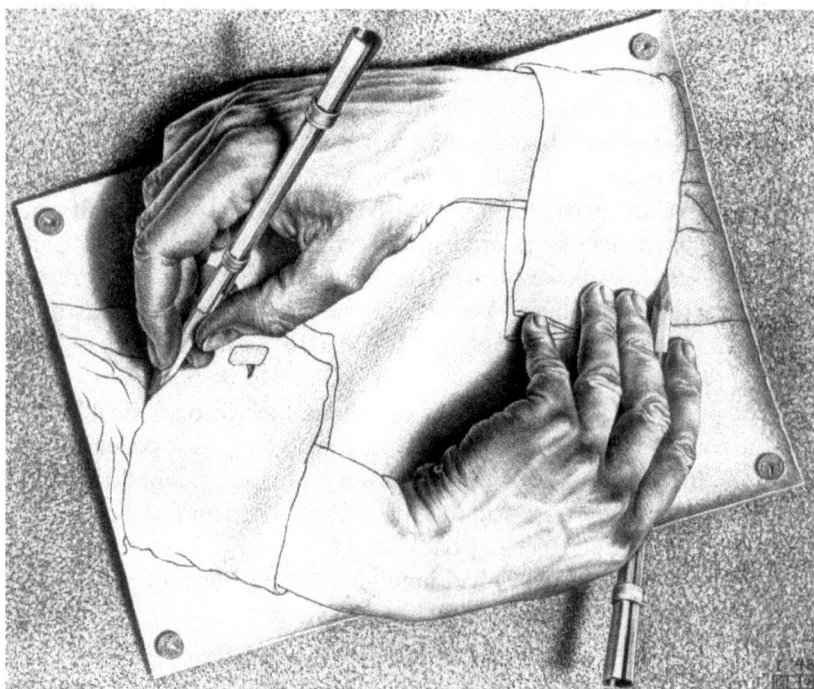

Maurits C. Escher. *Drawing Hands.* 1948

Afterword

Since the Foreword began with a Danish dream, it is fitting to close with a lucid dream.

Last night I fell asleep listening to an audio-book. (It's like someone reading a bedtime story.) In my dream a radio was blaring and I tried turning it off. I couldn't hear what people were saying. The world was in confusion. (Some of these audio-books are dramatized.) I turned the dial off, but the noise persisted. I pulled out the plug. The hectic racket continued. I couldn't hear myself think, and it seemed to be growing louder! In desperation I pulled out the batteries. The annoying radio continued blaring.

Suddenly, it dawned on me. "This is impossible. I must be dreaming," I said to my brother who was witnessing my predicament. He looked skeptical. "This is a dream," I concluded confidently. "Isn't it?" And I awoke.

The Einstein-Podolsky-Rosen paradox as well as the infamous "double-slit" experiment evoke feelings reminiscent of those I had in the lucid dream. Turning off the radio, unplugging it, pulling out the batteries—and yet it continued playing. The impossibility made me realize I was in a dream. In a similar manner, "E-P-R" and especially the "double-slit" give me the eerie, haunting suspicion that the universe is a "real" dream. "Isn't it?" Am I awake? Do thoughts and dreams mold the form of our universe? Is this all just a lucid, holographic dream?

Wayne Omura
Easter, 2015

"Let us admit what all idealists admit—the hallucinatory nature of the world. Let us do what no idealist has done—let us search for unrealities that confirm that nature. I believe we shall find them in the antinomies of Kant and in the dialectics of Zeno . . . 'The greatest wizard (Novalis writes memorably) would be the one who bewitched himself to the point of accepting his own phantasmagorias as autonomous apparitions. Wouldn't that be our case.' I surmise it is so. We (that indivisible divinity that operates in us) have dreamed the world. We have dreamed it as enduring, mysterious, visible, omnipresent in space and stable in time; but we have consented to tenuous and eternal intervals of illogicalness in its architecture that we might know it is false."

— Jorge Luis Borges

215. Jorge Luis Borges, "Avatars of the Tortoise" from Other Inquisitions as quoted by Michael Talbot, Mysticism and the New Physics (London: Penguin Books, Ltd, 1981, 1993), p. 1.

Afterthought

I must admit to a little trepidation about the premise of objective idealism as the universal substrate. If our thoughts shape reality then what happens when we die? A relative and a scientist friend told me they didn't believe in any form of existence after death. In their case, since that is what they believe, then their consciousness might just vanish. Another relative is a Christian. In her case, she might go to Heaven, or if she felt guilty, she would go to Hell.

Like the Tibetan Buddhists, I have the intuition that the after-life (if there is one) would be dream-like. If you can control the dreams then you control your experiences. But if you are fearful or undisciplined you may become lost in the dream world which can easily morph into a nightmare.

Maybe that dream or nightmare is the reality we now call life. Maybe it is all undifferentiated. Maybe we are already dead. Maybe the Universal Hologram is just projecting images from the past.

How would I know? I'm not dead (so far as I know). (Others might argue otherwise.) And I am not enlightened. I'm not even a scientist. Or even a Tibetan Buddhist. But I am a dreamer (albeit a woefully undisciplined one).

"Life is a dream... Realize it.." [216]

—*Sai Baba*

"This world is but canvas to our imaginations." [217]

—*Henry David Thoreau*

216. Abdelfattah Mohsen Badawi, <u>A Journey to Self-Peace</u> (North America & International: Trafford Publishing, 2012), p. 52.
217. Henry David Thoreau, <u>A Week on the Concord and Merrimack Rivers</u> (Boston: Houghton, Mifflin and Company, 1883), p.309.

About the Author

Wayne Omura lives and writes in Denver, Colorado. He is the author of *Movies and the Meaning of Life: The Most Profound Films in Cinematic History*, *Zen Foot-Notes: Upon the Unknown Passage*, and *Warriors of Life: The Martial Art of Existence*.